FW 190A, F, an[d] in a[c]tion

By Brian Filley
Color by Don Greer
Illustrated by Ernesto Cumpian and Richard Hudson

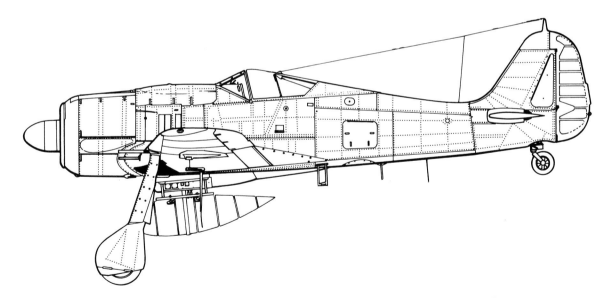

Aircraft Number 170

squadron/signal publications

Fw 190F-8s of Schlachtgeschwader 4 (*SG* 4) attack targets on the Eastern Front during the summer of 1944. The F-8 was the ground-assault counterpart to the popular Fw 190A-8 fighter. Black E displays an extensive interpretation of the unit's colors, while White F wears a more subdued variation.

Photo Credits

Hans Obert	E.C.P. Armee	
Hans Redeman	Richard F. Grant	Bob Hanes
Michael Schmeelke	Squadron Archives	Gene Stafford
Horvath via Stapfer	Imperial War Museum	USAF
R. Meixner	VFW-Fokker	Mihai Moisescu

Special Acknowledgements

A special thanks to the 'old crew' at LCN for all their moral and logistical support, especially Carolyn, Jackie, Jerry, Joey and Marcie, as well as many other friends too numerous to mention (you know who you are).

Dedication:

To my loving parents,
Marie F. Filley (1916—1967) and
Alfred W. Filley (1913—1993)
...together again.

ISBN 0-89747-404-X
If you have any photographs of aircraft, armor, soldiers or ships of any nation, particularly wartime snapshots, why not share them with us and help make Squadron/Signal's books all the more interesting and complete in the future. Any photograph sent to us will be copied and the original returned. The donor will be fully credited for any photos used. Please send them to:

Squadron/Signal Publications, Inc.
1115 Crowley Drive
Carrollton, TX 75011-5010

Если у вас есть фотографии самолётов, вооружения, солдат или кораблей любой страны, особенно, снимки времён войны, поделитесь с нами и помогите сделать новые книги издательства Эскадрон/Сигнал ещё интереснее. Мы переснимем ваши фотографии и вернём оригиналы. Имена приславших снимки будут сопровождать все опубликованные фотографии. Пожалуйста, присылайте фотографии по адресу:

Squadron/Signal Publications, Inc.
1115 Crowley Drive
Carrollton, TX 75011-5010

軍用機、装甲車両、兵士、軍艦などの写真を所持しておられる方はいらっしゃいませんか？どの国のものでも結構です。作戦中に撮影されたものが特に良いのです。Squadron/Signal社の出版する刊行物において、このような写真は内容を一層充実し、興味深くすることができます。当方にお送り頂いた写真は、複写の後お返しいたします。出版物中に写真を使用した場合は、必ず提供者のお名前を明記させて頂きます。お写真は下記にご送付ください。

Squadron/Signal Publications, Inc.
1115 Crowley Drive
Carrollton, TX 75011-5010

(Right) Quiet, for now... Factory fresh Fw 190A-5s of *Jagdgeschwader* 26 await combat action which is certain to come. France, summer, 1943.

INTRODUCTION

In September of 1941, mysterious, snub-nosed Luftwaffe fighters staked a claim to the skies over Dunkirk. Seizing control of the air from Britain's Spitfire Mk.V, these new fighters maintained a near stranglehold over Allied airpower until the summer of the next year. This new fighter, the Fw 190, which had been agreed to by the *Luftwaffe's* RLM (*Reichsluftfahrtministerium*/State Aviation Ministry) as a 'supplemental' fighter to the already proven Messerschmitt Bf 109, had instead demonstrated qualities which were arguably superior — stirring a debate which has outlived World War Two itself. Without question, however, the Fw 190 would become a critical factor in Germany's very survival during those terrible years of conflict, and still remains the most historically significant aircraft produced by the Focke-Wulf Flugzeugbau, G.M.B.H. and its chief designer, *Diplom Ingenieur* (Dipl. Ing - Certified Engineer — later Professor) Kurt Waldemar Tank. By the end of hostilities, on 8 May 1945, Germany's 'mystery fighter' had become for the Allies an all too common sight on every war front, and within the five years of war had been manufactured in numbers estimated at roughly 20,000 machines.

Originally, when the RLM requested design submissions for a 'back-up' fighter to the Bf 109 in late 1937, Kurt Tank's response was regarded with skepticism for two reasons. First, he had proposed a defensive air superiority fighter at a time when Germany's war planners were transfixed by purely offensive, tactical combat machines for rapid conquest. Secondly, Tank intended to power his design with an air-cooled radial engine, this being an affront to technical advisors who felt that only an in-line, liquid-cooled engine provided the needed horse power and aerodynamic design potential to suit the Luftwaffe's needs. Nevertheless, the RLM was intrigued by a fighter which would not further tax the foreseen demand for in-line engines and, by Tank's own assurance, could be easily produced by many sub-contractors. Subsequently, Tank was given the go ahead for project development, and the first technical drawings were prepared by Focke-Wulf's well organized draughtsmen by July of 1938.

The aircraft, designated the Focke-Wulf Fw 190, was a low-wing monoplane of all metal construction with fabric covered control surfaces. The pilot's cockpit was located close to the engine firewall and covered with a nearly all transparent, rearward sliding canopy which blended into the contours of the fuselage spine and provided excellent all round vision. Also, the Fw 190 was to be supported by outboard mounted wide track undercarriage legs with a total wheel track of 3,500mm (11.5 feet). Each inward retracting leg was electrically powered by separate motors, and ultimately proved to be extremely sturdy, despite its high stilt-like appearance.

Power was to be provided by a twin row, eighteen cylinder, 1,550 hp BMW 139 radial engine, produced by the Bayerische Moteren Werke, driving a three bladed VDM all metal propeller. Engine cooling was to have been maintained by a multi-bladed, compression producing fan at the mouth of the cowling, but due to delays with the fan's development, the first prototype was designed with a bullet shaped ducted spinner, which would create problems later.

The originally proposed armament (not fitted on the first prototype) was to be four synchronized machine guns (two 7.9mm MG 17 machine guns and two 13mm MG 131 machine guns), one of each to be mounted in each wing.

For ease of servicing the new fighter, Kurt Tank's design team incorporated a system of hinged panels which would easily expose every critical maintenance area, particularly the armament and powerplant. The panels themselves could be completely detached if needed.

Completed by the spring of 1939, the **Fw 190V-1** exemplified the clean, compact appearance

The Fw 190V-1 first flew on 1 June 1939. Until the planned cooling fan was ready the prototype was fitted with a large ducted spinner. The code letters (D-OPZE) were black and the new aircraft was camouflaged in Dark Green (RLM 71) and Black Green (RLM 70) splinter pattern on the upper surfaces over Light Blue (RLM 65) undersides. (Hans Redeman)

which the Fw 190 would maintain throughout its life. In keeping with the practice of the time, the prototype was finished in a camouflage of Black Green (RLM 70) and Dark Green (RLM 71) 'splinter' pattern on the upper surfaces, over Light Blue (RLM 65) under surfaces. A black swastika on a white circle on a red banner spanned the vertical tail, while the fuselage code, D-OPZE, was painted in glossy Black.*

The first flight of Fw 190V-1 took place on 1 June 1939 with Focke-Wulf chief test pilot, Hans Sander, being given the honor. Sander literally loved the handling displayed by the Fw 190, describing the aircraft's performance as *"delightful"* and light on the controls. Less delightful, however, was the tremendous amount of exhaust fumes and heat that filled the cockpit, grilling Sander with temperatures up to 130 degrees Fahrenheit! The RLM was pleased with the initial flight results, and development was allowed to proceed.

While metal was cut on a family of Fw 190 prototypes, flight testing of the Fw 190V-1 continued into the autumn of 1939, when it was transferred to the *Erprobungstelle* (E-Stelle - Testing Center) at Rechlin. Ultimately, the V-1 was fitted with its 10 bladed cooling fan along with the ducted spinner, but since the 'bullet nosed' spinner offered no substantial improvement in performance, the prototype was provided with a conventional spinner. In flight tests, the Fw 190V-1 was able to achieve a respectable speed of 594 km/h (369 mph), although engine over heating continued to be a problem. The Fw 190V-1, later coded W+FOLY,

*The German *Reichsluftfahrtministerium* (RLM) also established a set of standards for colors and markings used on Luftwaffe aircraft. German aircraft manufacturers were to adhere to a set of standard colors that were to be used on all German military aircraft. Each of the colors was assigned a name, e.g. *Schwarzgrun*, and a number, e.g. RLM 70. The Fw 190V-1 was officially painted in RLM 70 *Schwarzgrun* and RLM 71 *Dunkelgrun* on the upper surfaces, and RLM 65 *Hellblau* on the lower surfaces.

Fw 190V-1

V-1 w/ Ducted Spinner

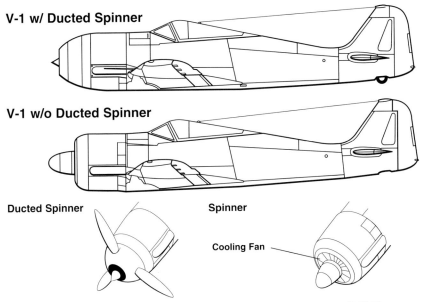

V-1 w/o Ducted Spinner

Ducted Spinner   **Spinner**

Cooling Fan

The Fw 190V-5 was the first machine to have the 1600hp BMW 801C engine installed. The heavier motor resulted in a substantial fuselage revision, moving the cockpit rearward to relocate the center-of-gravity. The V-5 originally had the smaller area wings, later replaced with larger wings under the designation V-5g.

FO+LY and finally RM+CA, continued to be used as a test airframe until 1943.

Due to frustrations with the 1550 hp BMW 139 powerplant, the next significant prototype, the **Fw 190V-5**, became the first machine equipped with a 1600 hp BMW 801C engine. Because of the weight of the new motor, which was approximately 160 kg (352 pounds) heavier, in order to maintain the center of gravity the fuselage was extensively redesigned, moving the pilot's cockpit rearward. The profile of the canopy was raised to provide an improved vision for the pilot and, thanks to the space created between the cockpit and engine cowling, provision was now made for a fuselage gun bay, with a rear and upward hinged access panel. Other details, such as a revision of the cowling contours and undercarriage doors, brought the Fw 190 closer to its production appearance.

During its test program the Fw 190V-5 was slightly damaged during a landing accident, providing Focke-Wulf engineers with the opportunity to equip the machine with a newly designed wing of increased span (from 31.4 feet to 34.65 feet) and increased surface area. With the installation of the new larger wing the original airframe was redesignated the **Fw 190V-5k** (*kleiner*/small) and the revamped airframe with the larger wing became known as the **Fw 190V-5g** (*grosser*/large). Later, the wings of the V-5 were used to conduct static wing loading tests.

By the end of 1939, the prototype testing program had accelerated rapidly, and of the first dozen *Versuch* aircraft (Research aircraft, of which there would be many throughout the war), most were used as test beds for engines (including some inline engines) and armament configurations. Over half of the Fw 190V-1 through V-13 aircraft were predesignated as 'pattern' airframes for the future pre-production Fw 190A-0 series and the initial production Fw 190A-1 series. In the event the Fw 190V-3 was never completed, being used as spare parts for other projects.

Fw 190A-0

By the beginning of 1940, tooling work for the pre-production Fw 190A-0s had been completed, 40 such machines being authorized by the RLM. Also, the larger, longer-span wings were ordered installed on all subsequent airframes, pending availability. As of prototype *Werke Nummer* (Work Number) 0015, the larger wings became standardized, only the initial *Versuch* aircraft and early A-0s (which sometimes were one-in-the-same) were built with short wings.

Throughout 1940, the details that would give the Fw 190A its personality were finalized. The

Fw 190V-5K

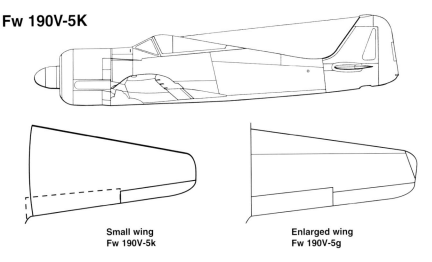

Small wing
Fw 190V-5k

Enlarged wing
Fw 190V-5g

A line-up of Fw190A-0 and *Versuch* aircraft including the dark camouflaged Fw 190V-1. By this time the V-1 had been equipped with an engine cooling fan and its code was changed to FO+LY.

Cockpit layout was extremely neat, with a unique split, staggered instrument panel and face up side consoles. The main radio apparatus was a *Funk Geräte* (Radio Device) FuG VIIa (also designated as FuG 7a), located within the aft fuselage. The antenna wire passed through the canopy, under tension, over a small pulley and was anchored to a small bulged fairing at the vertical tail tip.

All control surfaces were equipped with adjustable trim tabs (usually painted red) and the adjustable incidence horizontal tail was equipped with a small electrical motor located in the leading edge of the fin, powering a screw-jack when activated. The main wing flaps could be lowered to a maximum of sixty degrees, and were mechanically calibrated to be no more than a few degrees in variance of each other.

Ammunition for the fuselage mounted Rheinmetall 7.92mm MG 17 machine guns was contained in bins immediately below the weapons (900 rounds per gun) which could be removed through side-upper fuselage panels. The wing root MG 17s were fed from similar box containers, which could be removed via lower fuselage access panels. In the outboard wings, provisions were made for two drum fed 20mm Oerlikon MG FF cannons with hinged underwing access panels.

As engineers ironed out the bugs and flight testing continued at the factory level, a number of the earliest pre-production Fw 190A-0 machines were reserved for trials with various *Umrüst-Bausätze* (Factory conversions), which were identified with an additional 'U' designation. Eleven conversions labeled Fw 190A-0/U1 through Fw 190A-0/U11, were used for the exclusive testing of armament configurations, bombs and fuel drop tanks, external loads, and powerplants, including the new 1700 hp BMW 801D engine. While many of these test

engine cooling fan, now equipped with 12 blades, provided air for both the engine cylinders and the annular oil cooler and storage tank within the main forward cowl ring containing 55 liters (14.52 gallons) of lubricant. The two main fuselage fuel tanks (each containing a sealed electrical pump) were located in a boxed compartment below the pilot's floor board, and were accessible through removable ventral fuselage panels. The forward tank contained 232 liters (61.2 gallons) of fuel and the main rear tank contained 300 liters (79.25 gallons) of fuel, later adjusted to 292 liters (77 gallons) on subsequent combat variants. The oxygen supply was located in the aft fuselage, contained in three racks of tri-spherical steel bottles.

During tests, difficulties were encountered with release of the pilot's canopy for emergency bail-out above 250 mph, resulting in the installation of a jettisoning cartridge in the aft canopy. This was triggered by striking a lever above the canopy crank handle, located on the starboard side of the cockpit. On the port side of the fuselage, a tubular, retractable foot step and hatch covered hand-holds allowed the pilot to more easily board his machine.

When retracting or extending the undercarriage, the pilot was able to ascertain the position of his landing gear by observing a small red and white scaled indicator pin which projected through the wing upper surface just above each landing gear strut. Although the main gear was electrically operated, the tail gear was activated by a system of cables and pulleys connected to the main undercarriage and slid upwards into its well along an angled track. Maintenance access to the tail retraction mechanism was provided by a triangular hinged panel on the port side of the vertical tail fin. Standard tire dimensions remained the same throughout the Fw 190's career, the main tires being 700x175mm and the tail wheel being 350x135mm.

The pilot's stick and rudder controls were a push/pull rod and cable type, with differential bellcranks to smooth control of the rudder and elevators at higher speeds. Activation of the hydraulic braking system was achieved by the pilot's toe pressure on the rudder pedals.

Undercarriage Development

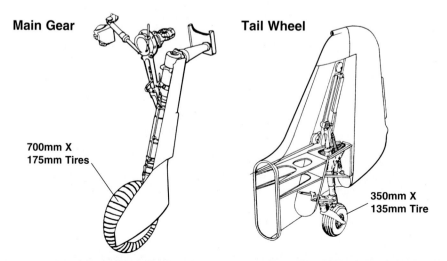

Main Gear

700mm X 175mm Tires

Tail Wheel

350mm X 135mm Tire

machines were finished in overall Gray (RLM 02), the Fw 190A-0s being prepared for service trials carried the standard day fighter camouflage of Gray Green (RLM 74) and Gray Violet (RLM 75) splinter on the upper surfaces over Light Blue (RLM 76)* undersides. The adjustable pitch VDM 9 metal propellers and spinners were normally finished in Black Green (RLM 70).

As preparations for full scale manufacturing continued, arrangements were made to form a trials unit at the *E-Stelle* at Rechlin, alternately referred to as *Eprobungsstaffel* 190 (Testing Squadron 190). In order to introduce the Fw 190 to combat pilots and create a pool of experienced personnel for further orientation, select pilots and groundcrew of II *Gruppe/Jagdgeschwader* 26 *Schlageter* were transferred from their base in Belgium to Rechlin in early 1941. By March of that year, the enthusiastic pilots were testing pre-production Fw 190A-0 aircraft, and some of the first production series Fw 190A-1s under simulated service conditions. Although some troublesome problems began to surface, the Fw 190 was about to embark on its eventful career.

Meanwhile, guided by the meticulous planning of Kurt Tank, a system of sub-contractors for Fw 190 production had been established. Among the many facilities which would ultimately participate in this massive effort (including a number of 'shadow factories' in German occupied countries), the main complexes had been tooled up at Arado (Warnemünde), AGO (Oscherleben) and, later, Fiesler (Kassel). These companies, together with the parent Focke-Wulf facility, would be joined by smaller contractors devoted to conversion work and repair as the war demanded.

* The official designation for RLM 76 was *Lichtblau*. Although both RLM 65 *Hellblau* and RLM 76 *Lichtblau* both translate into English as 'Light Blue' the two colors were different — RLM 76 having more of a lighter gray tint.

Fw 190A-0s were service tested at Rechlin with selected personnel of JG 26. This combat camouflaged A-0 has the initial production armament of four 7.92mm MG 17 machine guns and two outer-wing MG FF 20mm cannons. Early contours of the cowling blisters and panels are visible, as is the slightly smaller propeller spinner. (Meixner)

Fuel Tanks

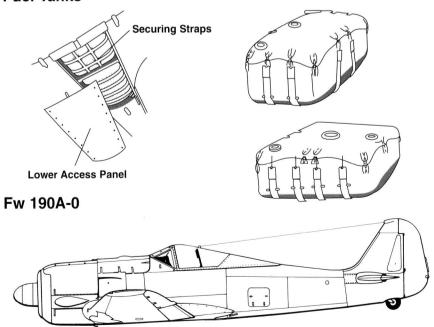

Securing Straps

Lower Access Panel

Fw 190A-0

A number of Fw 190A-0s were withheld for testing *Umrüst-Bausätze* (Factory Conversion sets). This overall RLM Gray A-0 has been fitted with a fuselage bomb load and appears to be updated with a forward cowl ring like the later production Fw 190A-1. (VFW-Fokker)

Development

Fw 190A-1

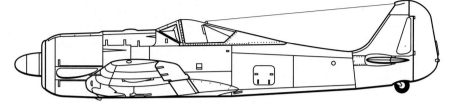

Fw 190A-2

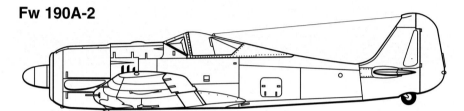

Fw 190A-3

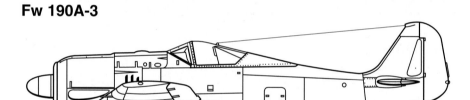

Fw 190A-4 (Early)

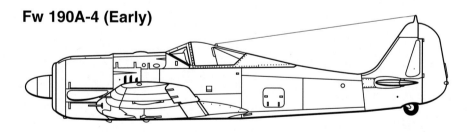

Fw 190A-5

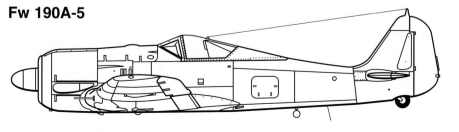

Fw 190A-6

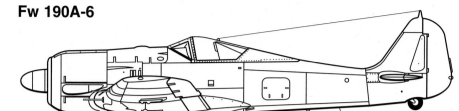

Fw 190A-7

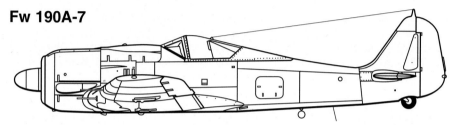

Fw 190A-8

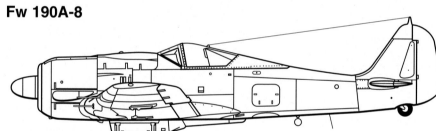

Fw 190F-8

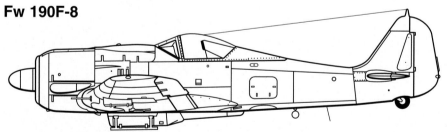

Fw 190G-8

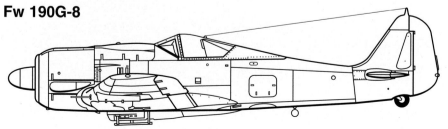

FW 190A-1

The first *Versuch* aircraft reserved as the prototype of the Fw 190A-1 series was the Fw 190V-7, its configuration of a BMW 801C engine, four MG 17 machine guns (two in the fuselage over the engine and one in each wing root), and two outer wing mounted MG FF cannons established the production pattern. Plans were being made to incorporate the faster firing 20mm Mauser MG 151/20E cannons into the Fw 190, but until these weapons were fully tested, ammunition stowage for the MG FF cannons was increased to 55 rounds per gun. To accommodate the larger ammunition drums, the hinged underwing armament panels were redesigned with a bulged shape.

The Fw 190A-1 was essentially similar to the pre-production A-0, but with a number of refinements. The cowling panels were redesigned for more efficient field servicing, and the cowling side blisters (which housed internal ducts to the supercharger and rear cylinder banks) were changed from a perfect 'tear drop' shape to one with a more flattened top. Steeply angled dual support rods were added to the pilot's 12mm armored headrest and the propeller spinner was slightly enlarged and elongated. Along with the main FuG 7 radio, provision was made for the installation of an FuG 25a IFF (Identification Friend or Foe) radio, which was detectable by a small whip aerial beneath the mid fuselage.

Although most Fw 190A-1s were equipped with the 1600 hp BMW 801C-1 powerplant, some were fitted with the 1700 hp BMW 801D. To achieve more efficient cooling of the more powerful engine, those machines powered by the BMW 801D were equipped with vertical cooling slots just behind the cowling on both sides of the fuselage. Sources indicate that the BMW 801D engines (D-1 and D-2 models) were installed depending on availability, and were retrofitted to earlier machines when possible.

During the spring of 1941 the first Fw 190A-1s joined the pre-production Fw 190A-0s in the field-evaluation program at *E-Stelle* Rechlin and the pilots of *Eprobungstaffel* 190. After concluding testing of the Fw 190 at Rechlin, the crews from II/JG 26 *Schlageter* were transferred to Le Bourget airfield in France for continued orientation. Unfortunately, problems persisted with the BMW powerplants, bordering on chaos; engine fires, fouled plugs, and vibration damage nearly led to the cancellation of the Fw 190 program by the RLM. Only determined talks between Focke-Wulf and BMW, with the assistance of Rechlin technical advisors, resulted in dozens of detailed modifications which satisfied the Fw 190's critics and earned final approval for full-scale production to resume.

Meanwhile, II *Gruppe*/JG 26 had begun a complete conversion from the Messerschmitt Bf 109E to the Fw 190, and by 1 September 1941, the Fw 190s were blooded in combat with Royal Air Force (RAF) Spitfire Mk. Vs over Dunkirk. With its superior speed, maneuverability, and rate of climb, the heavily armed Fw 190s of JG 26 had scored their first victories against a larger force of Spitfires without loss. So shocked were the RAF pilots, that their initial reports claimed that their radial engined adversaries were upgraded, ex-French Curtiss Hawk 75s! Fortunately for the RAF, engine problems left many of the Fw 190s unserviceable, but the Focke-Wulf's unquestionable mastery of the skies lived up to its nick name of *Würger* (Butcherbird or Shrike).

Sources vary on the exact number of Fw 190A-1s produced. Some state as few as 100 machines, however, later estimates claim over 400 were manufactured by Focke-Wulf, Arado and AGO before the changeover to production of the Fw 190A-2 was completed by early 1942.

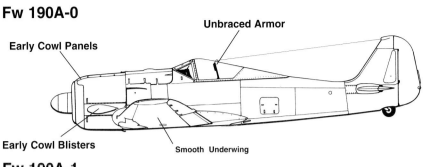

Fw 190A-0

Unbraced Armor · Early Cowl Panels · Early Cowl Blisters · Smooth Underwing

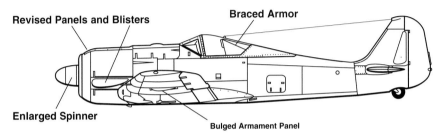

Fw 190A-1

Revised Panels and Blisters · Braced Armor · Enlarged Spinner · Bulged Armament Panel

Ready for action during the late summer of 1941. A typical feature of the Fw 190A-1 were the open wing root portals for the MG 17 machine guns. The slightly enlarged spinner of the A-1 is also visible, as well as the lack of cooling slots behind the cowling, indicating the more common BMW 801C engine.

Among the problems plaguing the Fw 190A-0 and A-1 during service orientation was engine overheating and fires, almost leading to the cancellation of the Fw 190 program. Cooling slots behind the cowl was part of the solution.

Red 1 (W.Nr. 027) was reportedly the aircraft of *Oberleutnant* Walter Schneider of II *Gruppe/JG* 26 — the nineteen tail victories were carried over from his Messerschmitt Bf 109. According to some sources, this aircraft was originally an Fw 190A-0 brought up to A-1 standards.

Despite being powered by a radial engine the sleek clean lines of the Fw 190A-1 are evident in W.Nr 033 of II *Gruppe/JG* 26. *Jagdgeschwader* 26 was the first unit to take the Fw 190 into combat, scoring three victories on 1 September 1941, with no losses.

W.Nr 027 receives fuel in one of its two starboard fuselage filling points. Just behind the mechanic is the oxygen filling point and the first aid panel is partially covered by the *Balkenkreuz*. One of the headrest support rods under the canopy is bent.

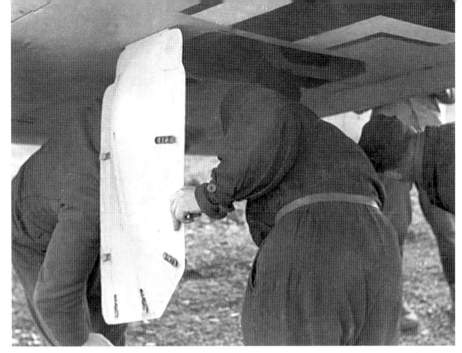

The outer underwing armament panels were hinged for easy access to the 20mm Oerlikon MG FF cannons. The bulged shape allowed clearance for the cannon's 55 round ammunition drum.

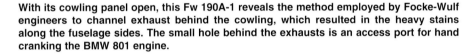

With its cowling panel open, this Fw 190A-1 reveals the method employed by Focke-Wulf engineers to channel exhaust behind the cowling, which resulted in the heavy stains along the fuselage sides. The small hole behind the exhausts is an access port for hand cranking the BMW 801 engine.

A pilot of II/JG 26 maneuvers into the cockpit and his parachute straps. The smooth wing root paneling and dual headrest supports are visible. The lack of cooling slots behind the cowling indicates a BMW 801C powerplant.

BMW 801 Engine

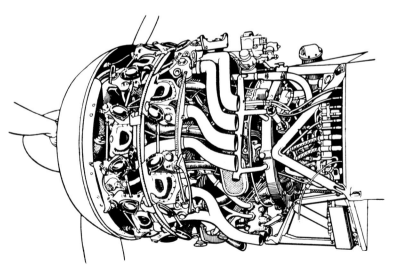

11

FW 190A-2

Essentially similar to the A-1 in appearance the Fw 190A-2's most distinguishing characteristic was the installation of two belt fed Mauser MG 151/20E 20mm cannons in the wing roots, replacing the 7.92mm MG 17 machine guns. To clear the larger cannon breeches, bulged doors were added to the upper wing root armament hatches, a feature the Fw 190 would retain for the remainder of its development. The fuselage mounted MG 17 machine guns were retained, as were the outboard MG FF cannons, however, the MG FF cannons were frequently removed to reduce weight and increase speed with pilots relying on the faster firing, more accurate MG 151s.

Like the Fw 190A-1, those Fw 190A-2s equipped with a BMW 801D engine featured cooling slots behind the engine cowling. In detail, the pilot's armored head-rest was now supported by a single flat brace, although a number of A-2s were still equipped with the dual rod head-rest braces. Again, an FuG 25 IFF radio could be installed, with its ventral 'whip' aerial in the same location.

Specifications of the BMW 801C equipped Fw 190A-1 and A-2 were comparable, with a maximum speed of 590 km/h (366.6 mph), a range of 1030 kilometers (640 miles) and an average loaded weight of 3400 kilograms (7495 pounds). With installation of the BMW 801D-1 or D-2 powerplant, weight was increased by roughly 600 pounds, and range being reduced by as much as 100 plus miles. Still, these detriments were offset by a respectable speed increase of 20-40 mph.

Entering production in August of 1941, the Fw 190A-2s joined the troubled Fw 190A-1s in combat service during the autumn of that year. Along with *JG* 26, other units employing the Fw 190 soon included *JG* 1, *JG* 2 and *JG* 5. *JG* 26 was entirely converted to the Fw 190 by early 1942. Fortunately the Fw 190A-2 benefitted by having the emergency modifications of the A-0/A1 incorporated into it on the assembly line, and with fewer problems, the Fw 190A-2 maintained the Focke Wulf's superiority over British airpower.

On 12 February 1942, Fw 190s participated in the epic air battle which developed above the famous 'Channel Dash' of the German warships *Gneisenau*, *Prinz Eugen*, and *Scharnhorst* from the French port of Brest.

Attacking RAF aircraft and Fleet Air Arm Fairey Swordfish torpedo bombers were severely mauled by defensive Luftwaffe 'top cover'. Most of the credit for the nearly fifty British aircraft destroyed went to the Fw 190. Simply put, the pilots of the RAF were able to score some victories over the Fw 190, but Kurt Tank's remarkable fighter had clearly become a thorn deeply imbedded in the RAF's side!

Production of the Fw 190A-2 began to taper off by mid-1942, being replaced on the assembly lines by the Fw 190A-3. Precise production figures of the A-2 are unknown, some sources quoting strangely similar totals for both the Fw 190A-1 and A-2 (possibly due to concurrent manufacturing). Figures of approximately 400 machines have been claimed, with others as high as 950. Some Fw 190A-2s were used as test beds for *Umrüst-Bausätze* (Factory Conversion) experimentation for future variants and accessory equipment.

This Fw 190A-2 has cooling slots, which ultimately became standard, but still features an early dual headrest support. Its outboard cannons have been removed and it is equipped with FuG 25 Identification Friend or Foe (IFF) radio (the aerial is visible below the aft fuselage).

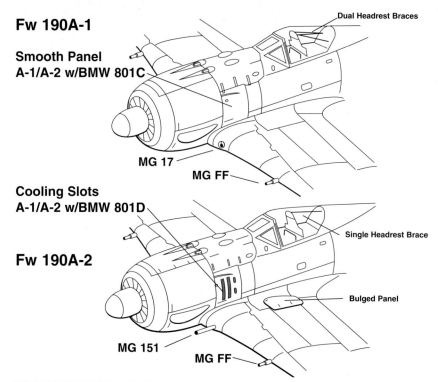

Fw 190A-1

Dual Headrest Braces

Smooth Panel
A-1/A-2 w/BMW 801C

MG 17

MG FF

Cooling Slots
A-1/A-2 w/BMW 801D

Single Headrest Brace

Fw 190A-2

Bulged Panel

MG 151

MG FF

These aircraft are Fw 190A-2s, as their 20mm inboard wing cannons indicate, yet none of them have cooling slots, indicating the use of a BMW 801C powerplant. Contrary to popular belief, the presence (or absence) of cooling slots is not a certain method of identifying the Fw 190A-1, A-2 or A3 variants.

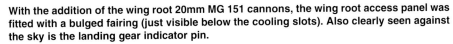

With the addition of the wing root 20mm MG 151 cannons, the wing root access panel was fitted with a bulged fairing (just visible below the cooling slots). Also clearly seen against the sky is the landing gear indicator pin.

Jagdgeschwader 2 was another unit which converted to the Fw 190 during late 1941 and early 1942. This A-2 has cooling slots and the single headrest support, which was more typical of late A-2s. The rudder and lower cowling are Yellow (RLM 27 *Gelb*), while the unit insignia and fuselage characters are white with black outlines.

Some early Fw 190s were sent to the Eastern Front for cold weather service evaluation and the harsh winter took its toll. This aircraft (an A-1 or A-2) has a later headrest support, but no cooling slots.

FW 190A-3

Due to the rapid development of the Fw 190, the first examples of the Fw 190A-3 were ready to leave the assembly lines by late 1941. The Fw 190A-3 was basically identical to the A-2, but standardized on the BMW 801D-1 and D-2 powerplants. As a result the forward fuselage cooling slots also became standard. Radio equipment and armament was the same as that found on the A-2, including the frequent removal of the outer wing mounted MG FF cannons for considerations of weight and speed.

With the introduction of the Fw 190A-3, approval was given for combat use of an optional ventral fuselage ETC 501 rack, which featured a long ventral fuselage fairing and allowed for carrying a 300 liter fuel drop tank or an optional bomb load (usually a single 250 kg/551 lb bomb or 500 kg/1,102 lb bomb). Carrying the bomb load, the Fw 190 could now serve as a *Jabo* (*Jagdbomber*/fighter bomber), capable of attacking ground targets and still easily capable of defending itself in dogfights. The carrying of a ventral fuselage load sometimes led to the removal of the inboard undercarriage doors, which would become an increasing practice on future Fw 190 variants. Later, those versions produced as dedicated weapons carriers would be manufactured with the inboard doors deleted completely.

Testing the various *Umrüst Bausätze* (factory conversion sets), which had received limited attention with the Fw 190A-2, was now accelerated with the A-3. Although some records disagree on the exact nature of these installations, as well as the frequency of their combat use, they would become instrumental in future Fw 190 development. Some of the most notable conversions for the Fw 190A-3 were as follows:

Fw 190A-3/U1 Some sources state that this was a dedicated fighter-bomber conversion, with outer wing MG FF cannons deleted and a ventral fuselage ETC 501 bomb rack installed. Others maintain that the test air-frame (coded PG+GY, W.Nr. 130270) served as a prototype for the future extended-fuselage Fw 190A-5 series.

Fw 190A-3/U2 An airframe used to test underwing, tube-launched RZ 65 anti-aircraft rockets. Not adopted for operational use.

Fw 190A-3/U3 Several test aircraft were produced for extended ground attack capability, including the ventral fuselage ETC 501 rack, optional small caliber underwing bomb racks, and tropicalized air intakes added to the cowling sides (a variation of the intakes described for the A-3/U7).

Fw 190A-3/U4 A reconnaissance conversion with the outer wing cannons deleted and up to two Rb 12 aerial cameras installed within the aft fuselage. The camera aperture was located under the aft fuselage, surrounded by a curved housing and splash guard. Optionally, a gun camera could be installed in the outboard leading edge of the port wing (an EK 16 or a BSK 16). Produced in limited numbers, this variant was reportedly used by the tactical operational training *Staffel*, 9./(H) Lehrgeschwader 2.

Fw 190A-3/U7 A special high altitude fighter conversion with armament reduced to the wing root MG 151 cannons and open faced intakes fitted to the cowling blister locations for greater air flow to the engine supercharger and rear engine cylinder banks. The use of these intakes would become standard on tropicalized variants and be seen more frequently on other Fw 190 variants.

Fw 190A-3s began to reach Western Front units by the spring of 1942, joining the Fw 190A-2s and allowing the earlier A-1s to be phased out of frontline service. The use of the Fw 190 was still only a trickle into service with units on the eastern front.

The Fw 190A-3 became the first variant to fall intact into British hands. During the evening of 23 June 1942, *Oberleutant* Arnim Faber, adjutant of III *Gruppe*/JG 2 *Richthofen*, had

Other than standardization on the BMW 801D engine the Fw 190A-3 was externally similar to the late Fw 190A-2. By now, the single brace for the headrest armor and the fuselage cooling slots were permanent fixtures.

The pilots of a *Staffel* along the Channel Coast prepare for a morning brief in front of their waiting Fw 190A-3s. With the A-3, removal of the outboard wing cannons to reduce weight and increase speed became a common practice.

A mechanic buttons up the cowling of a JG 2 Fw 190A-3. The inboard undercarriage doors were often closed when the aircraft was at rest; they could be hand secured into position by ground personnel.

The solution of painting dark panels behind the exhausts to disguise sooting led to a unique Luftwaffe unit insignia, the black and white cowling 'eagle' originated by JG 2 'Richthofen'. Many Fw 190s carried stylized panel flashes late into the war.

become disoriented following combat with RAF Spitfires over the English Channel and accidentally landed at RAF Pembrey, near Swansea. It was ironic that *Oblt.* Faber even performed a victory roll over the airfield before personally delivering the Fw 190's secrets to Allied Intelligence! Worse yet for the *Luftwaffe* the British were about to release another thoroughbred from the Supermarine stables, the Spitfire Mk.IX, which would quickly dull the Fw 190's edge in air supremacy

Production figures of the Fw 190A-3 are, again, contradictory. Some sources claiming approximately 500 machines being produced, while higher estimates claim over 200 were delivered in late 1941 and over 1,800 were delivered in 1942. It must be noted that an extremely efficient system of recycling was being established by Focke-Wulf to re-build earlier variants, war weary airframes, as well as battle damaged aircraft to updated versions. Since the end of the war, this rebuilding effort has contributed to the confusion surrounding exact production totals, as well as the *Werke Nummer* blocks assigned to completed aircraft.

Against normal German policy restrictions concerning new military equipment, approximately 60 (some sources state 75) Fw 190A-3s were sold to neutral Turkey in late 1942, along with replacement engines and weapons.

On 23 June 1942, *Oberleutnant* Arnim Faber of III *Gruppe/JG 2* accidentally landed in England after a dogfight with Spitfires. The 'cock's head' emblem was the unit's insignia. The rudder and lower cowling were yellow, not red as has been stated by some sources. With Faber's Fw 190, the Allies were able to dissect the first intact example of the new fighter.

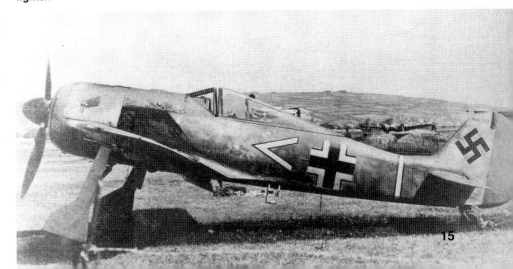

(Above) Removing the all metal VDM propeller for servicing was a relatively easy task, requiring little heavy equipment. With the cooling fan removed, the gear box housing of the BMW 801 engine is exposed.

(Above) Back in place, the propeller hub collars are tightened. The multi-bladed fan produced excellent air compression for cooling. The adjustable-pitch VDM propellers were finished in Black Green (RLM 70) at the factory while the cooling fan appears to be painted black.

(Left) *Major* Gerhard Schöpfel, *Kommodore* of JG 26, prepares for another mission in his Fw 190A-3. The yellow triangle under the cockpit designates fuel type (C3) and octane (100), while a black stencil indicates the rear fuel tank capacity of 292 liters. Barely visible is the Revi C12/D gunsight protruding through the instrument panel shroud. The canopy housing for the antenna wire pulley can be seen on top of the canopy.

The angry looking *Tatzelwurm* was the unit insignia of II Gruppe/JG 1 and was usually painted in the *Staffel* color, in this case red for the 5th *Staffel*. This Fw 190A-3, in need of an engine overhaul, is being prepared for towing by ground personnel. The foul weather tarp was standard issue with each Fw 190.

With towing cables in place and the tarp refastened, Red 2 is towed by a truck to a waiting maintenance hangar. The Fw 190 handbook specifically outlined proper towing procedures, whether by vehicle or ground crew. Usually, the castoring tail wheel was steered by a mechanic. The dark colors on the fuselage sides are where the factory delivered call signs have been painted out.

Towing Procedure

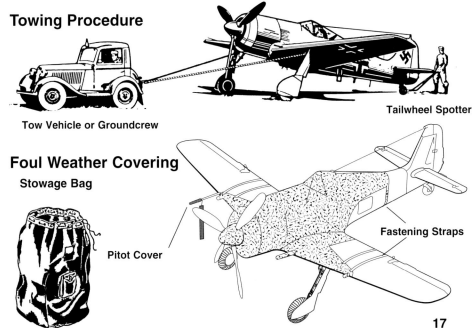

Tow Vehicle or Groundcrew

Tailwheel Spotter

Foul Weather Covering

Stowage Bag

Pitot Cover

Fastening Straps

With the advent of the Fw 190A-3/U3 factory conversion, the A-3 could take on the role of *Jabo (Jagdbomber)*. Black 34 is equipped with an ETC 501 fuselage rack, typified by a long ventral housing. A 300 liter fuel tank could also be carried in place of a bomb load.

A standard three-wheeled bomb trolley is used to raise an SC 250 (551 lb) bomb beneath an Fw 190A-3/U3. Normally when the *Würger* was used in the *Jabo* role, the outer wing MG FF cannons were removed, as were the inboard undercarriage doors.

The Fw 190A-3/U7 was a factory conversion to a high-altitude interceptor. The cowling air intakes allowed greater air flow to the supercharger and rear engine cylinder banks. This modification was found on subsequent Fw 190s on a limited basis.

FUSELAGE ETC 501 RACK

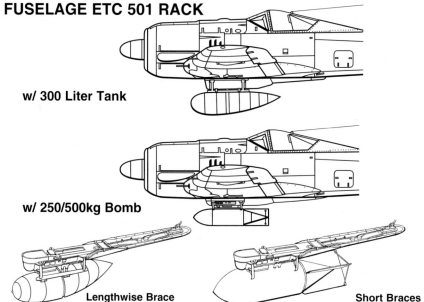

w/ 300 Liter Tank

w/ 250/500kg Bomb

Lengthwise Brace

Short Braces

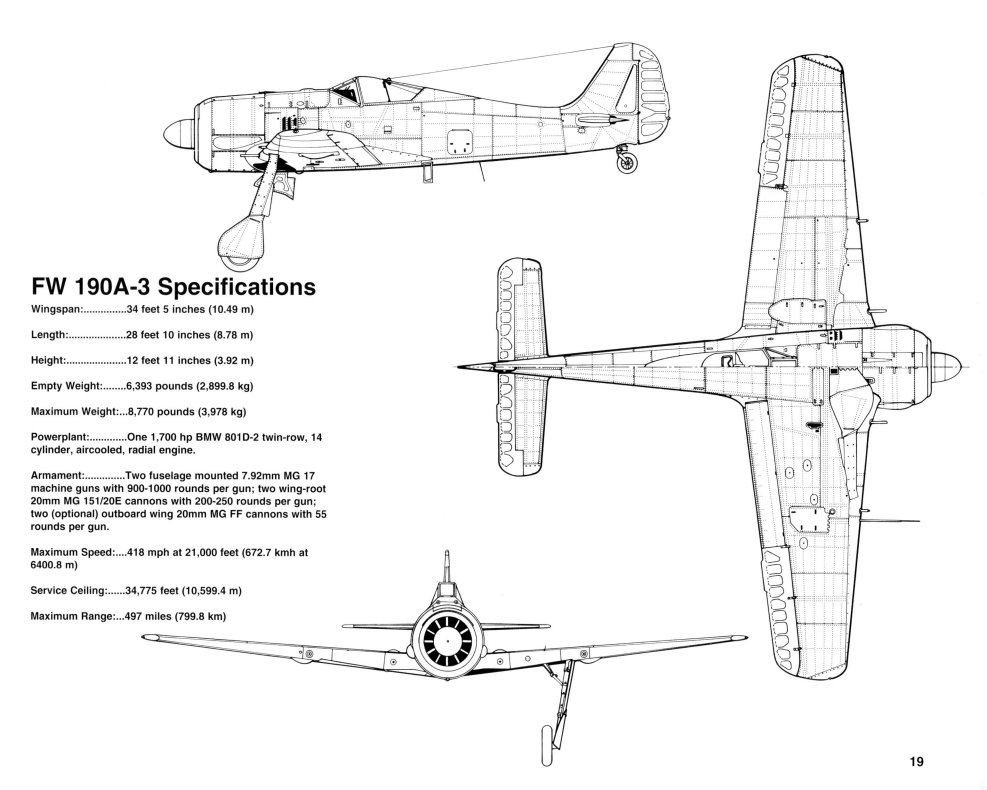

FW 190A-3 Specifications

Wingspan:...............34 feet 5 inches (10.49 m)

Length:....................28 feet 10 inches (8.78 m)

Height:....................12 feet 11 inches (3.92 m)

Empty Weight:........6,393 pounds (2,899.8 kg)

Maximum Weight:...8,770 pounds (3,978 kg)

Powerplant:.............One 1,700 hp BMW 801D-2 twin-row, 14 cylinder, aircooled, radial engine.

Armament:..............Two fuselage mounted 7.92mm MG 17 machine guns with 900-1000 rounds per gun; two wing-root 20mm MG 151/20E cannons with 200-250 rounds per gun; two (optional) outboard wing 20mm MG FF cannons with 55 rounds per gun.

Maximum Speed:....418 mph at 21,000 feet (672.7 kmh at 6400.8 m)

Service Ceiling:......34,775 feet (10,599.4 m)

Maximum Range:...497 miles (799.8 km)

FW 190A-4

The Fw 190A-4 was essentially the same as the Fw 190A-3, however, the main FuG 7 radio was replaced with an FuG 16 radio, resulting in the addition of a vertical antenna mast at the tip of the tail fin, as well as a revision of the aerials with an extra lead in wire to the upper aft fuselage. The optional FuG 25 IFF radio was retained, but due to internal upgrades, the ventral whip aerial was relocated further aft, although on some A-4s it could still be found in the forward position.

Similar to the Fw 190A-3, the A-4 was powered by a 1700 hp BMW 801D-1 or D-2 engines with the standard fuselage 'cooling slots'. On late series A-4 aircraft, however, adjustable cooling gills were to become more common, allowing the pilot to adjust the rate of airflow through the engine cowling. Some Fw 190A-4s were equipped with an MW 50 Methanol-Water engine boosting system for emergency power.

The pilot's 12mm armored headrest was substantially widened, although a number of early A-4s were still fitted with the slender headrest of the A-3. Conversely, some late model A-3s were equipped with the wider A-4 headrest, possibly as a retrofitting. On some very late model A-4s the perforated type of main wheel hubs were replaced with a solid design.

With the introduction of the Fw 190A-4 in early 1942, the Focke-Wulf was being transformed into a multi-role combat aircraft, thanks to the continuing research with factory conversions (*Umrüst-Bausätze*) and the establishment of field conversion sets (*Rüstsätzen*). Of the many conversions being made available, the most noteworthy were as follows:

Fw 190A-4/U1 A high speed fighter-bomber conversion with defensive armament reduced to the wing root cannons and the addition of an ETC ventral fuselage bomb rack. Night capability was enhanced with the addition of a port wing leading edge landing light and optional exhaust flame dampeners. This would account for the designation of some Fw 190A-4/U1's as *NachtJabos* (night fighter-bombers). A number of these night fighter-bomber aircraft are known to have operated with *SKG* 10 (*Schnellkampfgeschwader*/Fast Bomber Wing) for nocturnal harassment raids against England.

Fw 190A-4/U3 A ground assault variant with the outboard MG FF cannons deleted, inboard undercarriage doors removed, and a ventral fuselage ETC 501 rack fitted for the carrying of variable bomb loads. This included 250 kg (551 lb) and 500 kg (1100 lb) bombs, as well as the *Einhangerost* 4 (ER 4) multiple bomb pallet, which could carry four SC 50 (110 lb) bombs. Aircraft converted for this ground attack role saw combat with a number of units, and were the basis for the future Fw 190F-1.

Fw 190A-4/U4 A photo-reconnaissance version, like the Fw 190A-3/U4, with the outboard MG FF cannons removed and equipped with up to two internal, downward facing cameras, with aft ventral fuselage ports. The camera control box was mounted to a central cockpit pylon beneath the instrument panel and between the pilot's legs. Among the units known to have used this version operationally was 2.(*F*)/123, a long range reconnaissance *Staffel* operating for a time on the Western Front.

Fw 190A-4/U8 A high speed fighter-bomber with outboard MG FF cannons and, optionally, the fuselage MG 17 machine guns were removed. A fuselage ETC 501 rack was installed for the bomb load, while a 300 liter fuel tank was suspended beneath each wing on faired over Junkers designed mountings. These initial conversions (based on W Nr.669 and 670) formed the basis of the future Fw 190G *Jagdbomber-Reichweite* (*Jabo-Rei* - Long-range fighter-bomber) series. Fw 190A-4/U8s were issued in limited numbers to several units, including *SKG* 10 and some specialized units within *Kampfgeschwaders* (Bomber Wings). Combat radius was listed as 1600 km (994 miles).

***Rüstsätze* 1 (R1)** A field conversion set allowing for the installation of an FuG 16ZE radio, which was detectable by the addition of a ventral 'morane' type mast installed beneath the port fuselage wing root.

***Rüstsätze* 6 (R6)** Although its use would become more frequent as the war progressed, this conversion introduced the use of one tube launched *Werfer Granate* (*WGr.*) 21 (21cm) anti-aircraft rocket beneath each outer wing. These weapons proved to be effective against 'boxed' Allied daylight bomber formations.

Deliveries of the Fw 190A-4 began in June of 1942, ultimately serving with a greater number of units on all war fronts, particularly in the east against Russia. Among these units were *JG* 1, 2, 5, 11, 26, 51, 54, and *JG* 300. *Schlachtgruppen* (Ground-attack Groups) using the Fw 190 included *SG* 1, *SG* 2, *SG* 4, and *SKG* 10.

Despite increasingly superior Allied aircraft, Fw 190s continued to earn the respect of its

Tail Development

Fw 190A-3

Fw 190A-4

The Fw 190A-4 was externally identical to the A-3, however, with the change from an FuG VII radio to the FuG 16, the vertical tail antenna housing was replaced by an antenna post. With the introduction of the A-4, the Fw 190 would be seen in growing numbers on the Eastern Front.

adversaries as Luftwaffe pilots became more proficient with the *Würger*. Along with continual daylight fighter skirmishes, Fw 190 *Jabos*, based in France, flew cross-channel bombing raids against British airfields and cities by day and by night. While some Focke-Wulf units provided support for German forces in the see-saw battles of North Africa and the Mediterranean, the Eastern Front *Jagdgruppen* compiled impressive victories over all manner of Soviet ground forces and aircraft. Two of the most notable Eastern Front units were JG 51 *Mölders* and JG 54 *Grünherz* (Green Hearts), employing standard Fw 190 fighters, along with their bomb laden *Jabos* for any variety of missions.

Production of the Fw 190A-4 continued until early 1943, after some 900 aircraft were reportedly produced, possibly due in part to the remanufacture of earlier airframes.

Headrest Development

Fw 190A-3
early A-4

Fw 190A-4
some A-3's

Some of the most colorful Fw 190s were those of *JG* 54 *Grünherz* (Green Hearts) on the Eastern Front. This yellow-trimmed, snow camouflaged Fw 190A-4 has had its MG FF cannons removed, leaving the openings uncovered. The recharging cart is being used to replenish the aircraft's batteries.

Having hoisted the Fw 190A-4 into the firing position this Russian front ground crew prepares for weapons calibration. This heavily re-camouflaged aircraft features white unit markings, a yellow band behind the fuselage cross, and two low visibility numbers for identification (a small 5 on the cowling and a 2 on the wing leading edge). Also visible is the larger armored headrest and the wing root armament panel in the raised position.

During the warm weather months of 1943, Fw 190A-4s of *JG* 54 carried Black Green/Dark Green bomber camouflage. The canopy frame of this Fw 190A-4/U3 *Jabo* has been left in the original factory gray color.

21

The Fw 190A4/U3 could carry a variety of weapons. This green camouflaged aircraft of *JG 51 Mölders* is loaded with an AB 500 small weapons dispenser. The slightly dropped flaps and raised elevators were often seen on the Fw 190 at rest.

A pilot of *JG* 26 adjusts his chute harness in front of his early Fw 190A-4. Most A-4s featured the wider headrest armor (also fitted to some A-3s) and the FuG 25 IFF aerial was relocated further aft. However, some A-4s carried it in the original forward position.

A late model Fw 190A-4 of *JG* 2 suffered a headstand, wrapping its shredded tire around the port wing undercarriage indicator pin. This photograph provides a view of seldom seen upper surface details including the MG 17 blast troughs, later cooling gills, the bulged wing root armament panels, as well as the camouflage pattern. (Zdenek Titz)

Cooling Slot Development

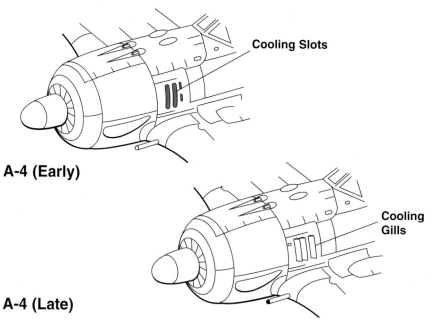

Cooling Slots

A-4 (Early)

Cooling Gills

A-4 (Late)

The Fw 190A-4/U4 was a factory converted photo reconnaissance variant, the underside aperture housing being just visible below the red number 6. Typical of early production A-4s, this aircraft of 2.(*F*)/123 has cooling slots behind the cowling.

Photo Reconnaissance Variants

Fw 190A-3/U4

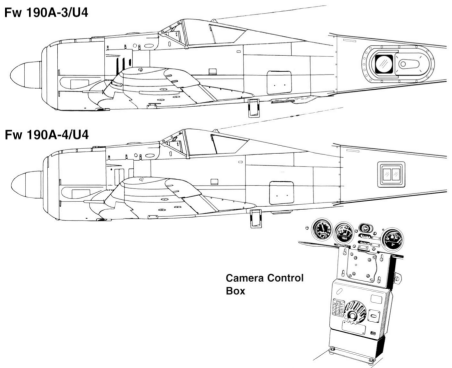

Fw 190A-4/U4

Camera Control Box

A mechanic steers the tail wheel of an Fw 190A-4/U4 of 2.(F)/123 with a tow bar. For better concealment, aircraft of this unit had their yellow rudders and lower cowlings over sprayed with differing patterns of Dark Gray mottling. Uniformly, Fw 190s were equipped with a 350x135mm rear tire.

III *Gruppe/SKG* 10 operated Fw 190A-4 *Jabos* during the battle for Tunisia. The crewman riding the wing is directing the pilot around potential obstacles, a common safety practice. (Mihai Moisescu)

23

In July of 1943, an Fw 190A-4/U8 force landed at Malling, in England. Its 300 liter wing mounted fuel tanks were removed prior to its evaluation. 5./*KG* 10, a *Schnellbomber Staffel* (fast bomber *Staffel*), conducted harassment raids with Fw 190A-4/U8s and the lesser known A-4 *Nacht-Jabo* variants. (Imperial War Museum)

The Fw 190A-4/U8 factory conversion saw considerable action with several units. It was the first variant fitted as a *Jabo-Rei* (*Jagdbomber-Reichweite*/Long-Range Fighter-Bomber), with a fuselage ETC 501 bomb rack and two Junkers-designed faired underwing mounts for 300 liter fuel tanks. (VFW-Fokker)

Part of Kurt Tank's design principal was ease of field maintenance, as demonstrated by this Fw 190A-4/U3 *Jabo* conversion. *Rüstsätze* 1 also allowed for the installation of an underwing *morane* mast for the improved FuG 16ZY radio option. The full designation of this machine was Fw 190A-4/U3/R1. This machine carries the early narrow type of head-rest armor found on some early A-4s.

Rüstsätze Conversions

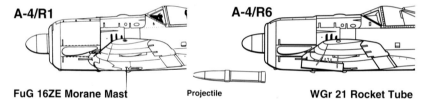

A-4/R1   A-4/R6

FuG 16ZE Morane Mast   Projectile   WGr 21 Rocket Tube

With the R6 field conversion, a single *WGr.* 21 (21cm) rocket tube could be hung beneath each wing. This effective anti-bomber formation weapon was used extensively on subsequent Fw 190 variants.

FW 190A-5

Even as the Fw 190A-4 was leaving the assembly lines, preparations were being made, in late 1942, for the introduction of the Fw 190A-5. This variant, with a number of detailed refinements, was to be even more adaptable to conversion sets for a number of differing combat roles.

Physically, the Fw 190A-5 was similar to the A-4, but to improve the center-of-gravity and reduce vibration, the engine and cowling were extended forward by 152.5mm (approximately 6 inches). This required lengthening the fuselage upper armament panel and forward fuselage, as well as the addition of a curved fillet installed immediately in front of the wing roots.

Further details were added, including structural modification of the rudder, an upward repositioning of the port fuselage radio access hatch, and standardization of the adjustable fuselage engine cooling gills. Due to internal equipment upgrades, including storage of the pilot's spherical oxygen containers, the port side first aid compartment was relocated further aft. The solid main wheel hubs, which had been seen on late production Fw 190A-4's, would be gradually standardized on the A-5. For high altitude operations air intakes for supercharger air flow (like those fitted to the Fw 190A-3/U7) were installed on the cowling side bulges on some A-5s.

Defensive armament remained the same as the Fw 190A-4 (two MG 17s, two MG 151 cannons, and two MG FF cannons), however, the outboard MG FF cannons were often removed depending upon operational needs. The ventral fuselage ETC 501 rack could be installed to carry a bomb load or a 300 liter drop tank, this being randomly substituted by the addition of a simplified fuel tank rack which had been developed for dedicated fighter variants. Provisions were also made for the installation of two ETC 50 bomb racks beneath each outer wing for carrying four 50 kg (110 lb) bombs, although this 'straight option' was fairly limited in use. Unlike the streamlined ETC 50 racks seen on later ground-attack variants of the Fw 190, these racks were often unfaired, such as those seen on Luftwaffe dive bombers like the Junkers Ju 87B/R *Stuka*. With the outer wing MG FF cannons removed, a gun camera (EK 16 or BSK 16) could be installed in the outboard leading edge of the port wing.

Extensive tests were conducted with the Fw 190A-5 employing the MW 50 Methanol-Water engine boost system, as well as the GM 1 nitrous-oxide power boosting system. When employed, these units provided added power to the 1700 hp BMW 801D-2 engine for short periods of advantageous speed. Unfortunately, technical problems hampered development of the GM 1 system, forestalling its service introduction.

Numerous conversion sets were tested on the Fw 190A-5, some of which were operationally employed. Most were *Umrüst-Bausätzen* (factory conversion sets) with at least two *Rüstsätzen* (field conversions) being provided, as follows:

Fw 190A-5/U1 Armament test bed for two Rheinmetall-Borsig 30mm MK 103 cannons in underwing trays. Problems with this system delayed its development.

Fw 190A-5/U2 A *Nacht Jabo-Rei* (night long-range fighter-bomber) with elliptical exhaust flame shields on the forward fuselage, a landing light and gun camera installation mounted in the outer port wing, and provision for one 300 liter fuel tank beneath each wing. An ETC 501 fuselage rack was fitted for bomb carrying. The MG FF cannons were deleted.

Fw 190A-5/U3 A ground-attack variation eliminating the outboard wing cannons and providing a fuselage ETC 501 centerline rack for bomb loads. Cowling air intakes with tropical filters were provided as an option. These conversions were operationally deployed, serving as the forerunner of the Fw 190F-2 series.

Fw 190A-5/U4 A proposed photo-reconnaissance variant similar to the A-3/U4 and A-4/U4.

The Fw 190A-5 differed from the A-4 in having the engine bearers and fuselage extended 152.5mm (approximately 6 inches) to correct the center-of-gravity and reduce vibration. The forward wing root fillet of this extension is visible, as are the opening/closing fuselage cooling gills which now became standard.

It may have been only six inches, but the extended fuselage of the Fw 190A-5 created a visual difference that was aesthetically pleasing. The upper armament panel of the 7.92mm machine guns was also lengthened.

Camera options were to include the Rb 12, Rb 20/30, Rb 50/30 and Rb 75/30 in downward facing mounts.

Fw 190A-5/U7 An armament test bed for two external 30mm MK 103 cannons, or two internal 30mm MK 108 cannons.

Fw 190A-5/U8 Another *Jabo-Rei* (long range fighter-bomber), similar to the the Fw 190A-4/U8, with reduced armament and 300 liter underwing fuel tanks. Sources indicate that airframes of this type were later redesignated as Fw 190A-5/U2s.

Fw 190A-5/U9 Armament test beds for the larger caliber fuselage mounted 13mm MG 131 machine guns, serving as prototypes for the later Fw 190A-7 and A-8.

Fw 190A-5/U10 Several armament test beds produced by the AGO facility, replacing the outboard wing MG FF cannons with MG 151/20E cannons, served as prototypes for the Fw 190A-6 series.

Fw 190A-5/U11 Armament test beds for external/internal mountings of the 30mm MK 103 and MK 108 cannons.

Fw 190A-5/U12 Armament test beds coded BH+CC (W.Nr. 813) and BH+CD (WNr. 814) for the installation of one *Waffenbehalter* (weapons container) WB 151 beneath each wing. Each container housed two 20mm MG 151/20E cannons with 145 rounds per gun. Although operational use was greatly restricted, this weapons arrangement was later provided as *Rüstsätze* 1 (R1) for later Fw 190A variants.

Fw 190A-5/U13 Another test airframe for a *Jabo-Rei*, similar to the A-5/U8 and reportedly served as a prototype for the Fw 190G series.

Fw 190A-5/U16 An armament test bed, again for wing mounted 30mm MK 103 and MK 108 cannons.

Fw 190A-5/U17 A ground attack variant with the outboard MG FF cannons deleted and a fuselage ETC 501 rack for large caliber bombs installed on the centerline. Four under wing ETC 50 bomb racks, with streamlined fairings, were installed on the wings to carry four 110lb SC 50 bombs. It was also tested with tropicalized cowling intakes. One machine, coded KO+ND, served as a forerunner to the Fw 190F-3/R1 series.

Rüstsätze 1 (R1) Installation of an FuG 16ZE radio (like the Fw 190A4/R1).

Rüstsätze 6 (R6) Installation of one *WGr.* 21 anti-bomber rocket tube beneath each wing (similiar to the Fw 190A-4/R6).

The Fw 190A-5, like its predecessor the A-4, quickly found itself on the inventories of *Jagdgruppen* on all fronts, particularly at a time when the fortunes of war were beginning to turn against Germany and its allies. Production of the Fw 190A-5 tapered off in late 1943, being supplanted by the Fw 190A-6. At least one example of the A-5 was supplied to Japan for evaluation. The Fw 190 was not adopted for Japanese use, however, the Allies nevertheless assigned the Japanese Fw 190 the identification code-name of Fred.

The Fw 190A-5 could be equipped with underwing ETC 50 bomb racks as a straight option. This early installation consisted of unfaired racks (two beneath each wing) like those fitted to the Ju 87B/R Stuka dive-bomber. Four 50kg (110lb) bombs could be carried.

Fuselage Development

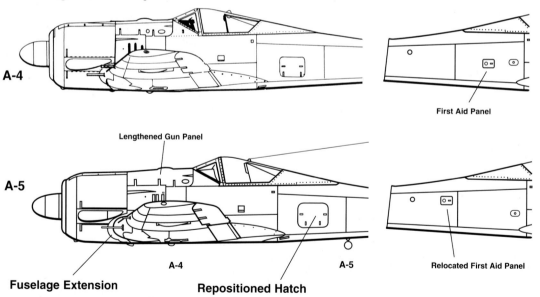

A-4

First Aid Panel

Lengthened Gun Panel

A-5

Fuselage Extension

A-4

A-5

Repositioned Hatch

Relocated First Aid Panel

Simplified Fuel Tank Rack

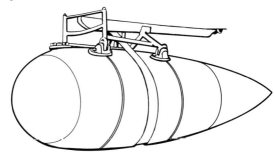

(Right) Similar to the Fw 190A-4/U8, the Fw 190A-5/U2 was a *Nacht Jabo-Rei*. It featured exhaust glare shields, an outer port wing mounted gun camera and landing light, an ETC 501 fuselage rack and two 300 liter long range fuel tanks. The tanks were mounted on N-braced racks designed by Messerschmitt, which were less bulky than the Junkers style faired racks. (Meixner)

(Below) Major Josef 'Pips' Priller arrives in his BMW Roadster for a mission in his BMW powered Fw 190A-5! Priller was a rather short, jovial man who achieved fame as one of only two pilots to attack the Allied invasion forces on 'D-Day', 6 June 1944. He flew this A-5 variant in 1943, equipped with the randomly used simplified fuel tank rack beneath the fuselage.

(Below) The elliptical exhaust shields blocked the glare of the exhausts from the pilot's view. (Meixner)

The Fw 190A-5/U3 was a factory *Jabo* conversion, with an added ETC fuselage rack and the outer wing MG FF cannons removed. Also visible are the revised and simplified main wheels and a port wing outboard gun camera, the most common position for this accessory on early Fw 190's.

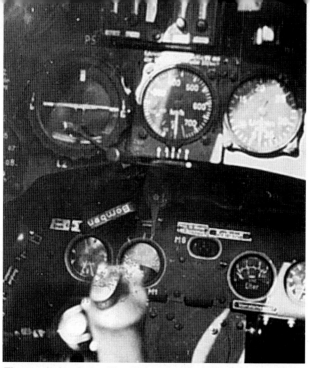

The cockpit of the Fw 190 *Jabo* featured two staggered instrument panels. This *Jabo* cockpit has a red release handle (above the control stick) marked *Bomben*. (Michael Schmeelke)

Cockpit

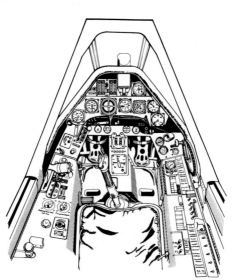

Armored Seat

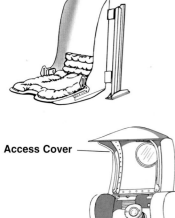

WB 151 *Waffenbehalters* (weapons containers) were originally tested on the Fw 190A-5/U12 factory conversion. Each tray held two belt fed MG 151/20mm cannons with 145 rounds per gun. Later designated as *Rüstsätze* 1, this weapons package saw only limited use. (Hans Redeman)

Access Cover

Wing Leading Edge Camera

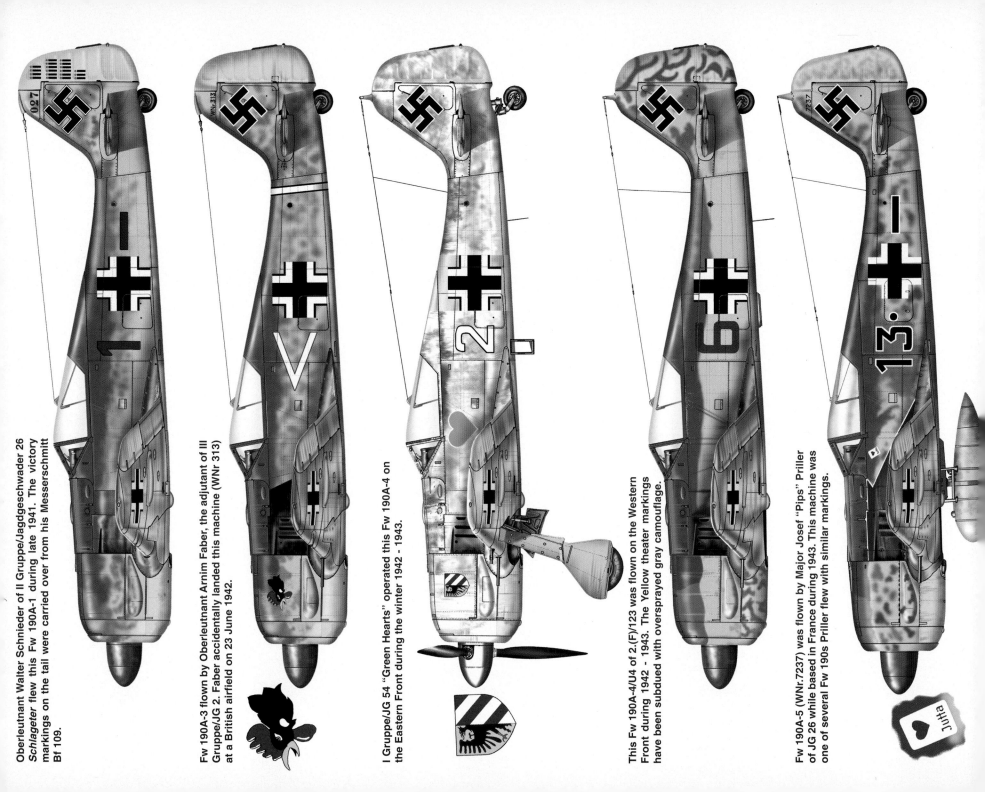

Oberleutnant Walter Schnieder of II Gruppe/Jagdgeschwader 26 *Schlageter* flew this Fw 190A-1 during late 1941. The victory markings on the tail were carried over from his Messerschmitt Bf 109.

Fw 190A-3 flown by Oberleutnant Arnim Faber, the adjutant of III Gruppe/JG 2. Faber accidentally landed this machine (WNr 313) at a British airfield on 23 June 1942.

I Gruppe/JG 54 "Green Hearts" operated this Fw 190A-4 on the Eastern Front during the winter 1942 - 1943.

This Fw 190A-4/U4 of 2.(F)/123 was flown on the Western Front during 1942 - 1943. The Yellow theater markings have been subdued with oversprayed gray camouflage.

Fw 190A-5 (WNr.7237) was flown by Major Josef "Pips" Priller of JG 26 while based in France during 1943. This machine was one of several Fw 190s Priller flew with similar markings.

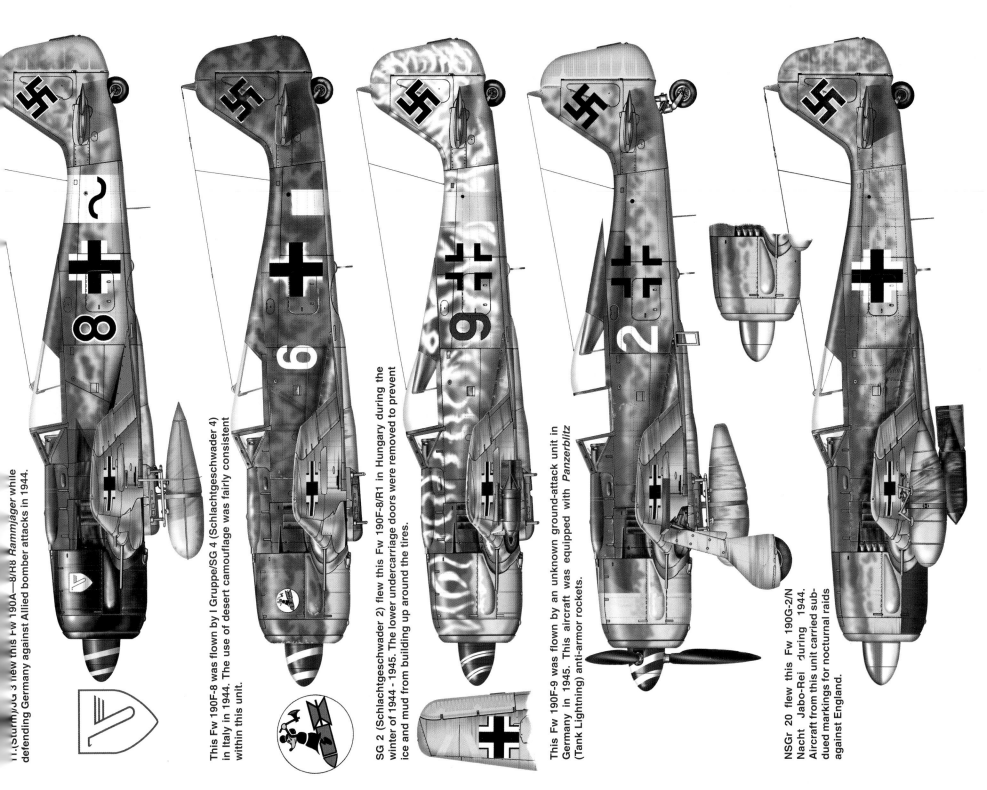

11.(Sturm)/JG 3 flew this Fw 190A—8/R8 *Rammjäger* while defending Germany against Allied bomber attacks in 1944.

This Fw 190F-8 was flown by I Gruppe/SG 4 (Schlachtgeschwader 4) in Italy in 1944. The use of desert camouflage was fairly consistent within this unit.

SG 2 (Schlachtgeschwader 2) flew this Fw 190F-8/R1 in Hungary during the winter of 1944 - 1945. The lower undercarriage doors were removed to prevent ice and mud from building up around the tires.

This Fw 190F-9 was flown by an unknown ground-attack unit in Germany in 1945. This aircraft was equipped with *Panzerblitz* (Tank Lightning) anti-armor rockets.

NSGr 20 flew this Fw 190G-2/N Nacht Jabo-Rei during 1944. Aircraft from this unit carried subdued markings for nocturnal raids against England.

Fw 190A-5/U3 *Jabos* were used for cross channel harassment raids against England. This aircraft has been credited to different units, including *JG* 26 and *JG* 54. Fittingly, the aircraft in this specialized bombing *Staffel* were decorated with a small bomb insignia on the aft fuselage. The cowling undersides and rudders were yellow.

The only variation in the markings of this *Jabo Staffel* was the aircraft number, all of the black fuselage characters were thinly out-lined in white. At the tip of the chevron is the first aid compartment, relocated on the Fw 190A-5 due to internal upgrades.

Main Wheel Development

Within minutes the ventral ETC 501 rack could be removed if the machine was needed as a dedicated fighter. The hastily patched over outer wing cannon position and missing inboard undercarriage doors indicate the ex-*Jabo* condition of this Eastern Front Fw 190A-5. The perforated main wheel hubs were gradually replaced by solid hubs on later A-5s.

Perforated

Fw 190A-4 and Early A-5s

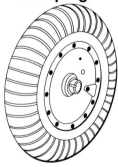

Solid Sheet Stamping

Fw 190A-5 and Late A-4s

Cowling Development

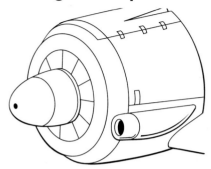

Optional Ram Super Charger Intake

Fw 190A-3/U7 and later variants

Optional Tropicalized Intakes

(Fw 190A-3s and later variants)

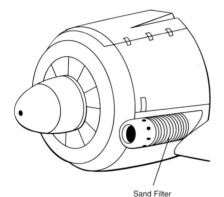

Sand Filter

KO+ND was reportedly an Fw 190A-5/U17 which served as the prototype for the Fw 190F-3/R1 Trop. It was a ground-attack version with a fuselage ETC 501 rack, four faired ETC 50 wing racks, and cowling intakes with sand filters. (Hans Redeman)

NC 900

In a twist of fate, the Fw 190A-5 would continue to see production and service even after the defeat of the Third Reich. Among the many 'shadow factories' which had been organized by Kurt Tank under the Focke-Wulf umbrella (including Posen, Cottbus, and Sorau), an underground facility had been established as SNCA du Centre (S.N.C.A.C.) at Cavant, France. In an effort to rebuild France's Armee de l'Air following the war, 64 Fw 190As were assembled by SNCA under the designation NC 900. Ironically, the principal unit which was briefly equipped with the NC 900 was GC 111/5 Normandie Niemen, the famous French volunteer unit which had battled Germany's Luftwaffe as part of the Soviet Air Force on the Eastern Front.

Production of the NC 900 was terminated in early 1946 and the service life of the NC 900 lasted only for as long as the Armee de l'Air needed to reorganize with up-to-date aircraft.

The Fw 190A-5 (and some A-8s) were produced in post-war France by SNCA, a previously established Focke-Wulf 'shadow factory' located at Cavant, France. Production ended in 1946 after 64 machines had been manufactured. Service use was limited. (Paul Camilio)

FW 190A-6

The Fw 190A-6 was developed in response to the detrimental weight escalation which had been placed upon the Fw 190's airframe due to constant upgrading (now up to 9138 lbs). A revised wing was developed, affording not only greater strength, but increased firepower as well. It was also decided that greater versatility in combat could be maintained by relying more on *Rüstsätzen* (field conversion sets) than factory modifications.

The Fw 190A-6 was essentially similar to the Fw 190A-5, however, wing armament was improved by the replacement of the outboard, drum fed 20mm MG FF cannons with belt fed Mauser MG 151/20mm cannons with 125 rounds per gun. Other notable differences were the longer barrels of the MG 151 cannons and underwing armament access panels with a smaller streamlined bump and spent casing chutes which replaced the shorter barrels and bulged armament panels of the MG FF cannons. The remaining armament of two fuselage mounted 7.92mm MG 17 machine guns and two wing root 20mm cannons remained unchanged.

Availability was reserved for the use of a GM-1 nitrous-oxide boosting system, or the more often used MW 50 methanol-water boosting system for emergency power. Minor details included the later addition of an under fuselage D/F loop for the FuG 16ZY radio (which was retrofitted to the Fw 190A-5) and the repositioning of the optional port wing gun camera which was moved further inboard on the wing leading edge between the wing-mounted cannons.

A variety of weapons and fuel tank packages could be carried on the optional fuselage ETC 501 rack with the inboard undercarriage doors removed. However, a number of Fw 190A-6s reached service units as pure interceptors, without the fuselage rack and the inboard wheel doors retained. Several *Rüstsätzen* were experimented with, but most would see only limited use. The most notable were:

Rüstsätze 1 (R1) Two underwing WB 151 weapons containers, each with two MG 151/20E 20mm cannons with 125 rounds per gun (other sources stating up to 145 rounds per gun). This conversion was based on the Fw 190A-5/U12 factory conversion, again seeing limited use due to the increased weight and drag produced by these units.

Rüstsätze 2 (R2) Alternate sources state that the *R2* conversion was reserved for the installation of outboard 30mm MK 108 cannons (which it later would be). However, it has also been maintained that the R2 designation was at this time assigned to the installation of increased fuselage fuel capacity in conjunction with the mounting of an underside 300 liter fuel tank.

Rüstsätze 3 (R3) Installation of long-barreled 30mm MK 103 cannons mounted in under wing pods (one per wing) with 32 rounds per gun. Again, this modification was extremely limited due to its detrimental effect on performance, as well as the fact that test results were inconclusive on the effectiveness of the weapon in combat.

Rüstsätze 6 (R6) Two under wing tubes for *WGr.* 21 (21cm) anti-bomber rockets, usually with the outboard wing guns deleted. This weapon was the same as that fitted to the Fw 190A-4/R6 and A-5/R6 and saw widespread use.

Although Fw 190A-6s would be assigned to various *Jagdgruppen* on Germany's war fronts, the majority of them operated in the West, particularly in Defense of the Reich from Allied bomber formations. Production of the Fw 190A-6 had commenced in June of 1943 and sources again differ on the number produced, most recent sources claiming approximately 3200 machines.

Due to weight escalation, the Fw 190 A-6 was introduced in 1943 with structurally strengthened wings which featured a belt fed MG 151/20mm cannon in the outboard wing position, replacing the drum fed MG FF cannon. The inboard cannons and fuselage 7.92mm MG 17 machine guns remained unchanged .

Wing Development

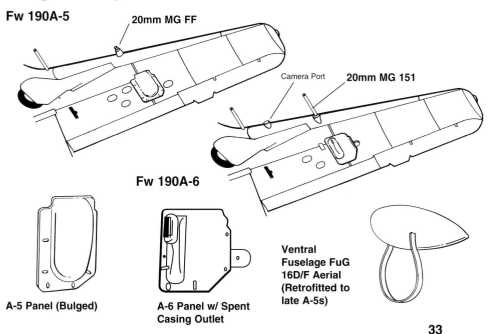

Fw 190A-5 20mm MG FF

Camera Port **20mm MG 151**

Fw 190A-6

A-5 Panel (Bulged)

A-6 Panel w/ Spent Casing Outlet

Ventral Fuselage FuG 16D/F Aerial (Retrofitted to late A-5s)

With its increased firepower, the A-6 was issued largely to Western Front interceptor units for the defense of Germany against Allied bombers. Yellow 1 is believed to have operated with *JG* 26, and is equipped with inboard undercarriage doors normal for an air superiority *Würger.*

FW 190A-7

As originally conceived, the Fw 190A-7 was to be produced as a dedicated high speed photo reconnaissance version, however, the shifting war situation dictated a greater need for the unabated production of fighter and ground-assault versions. In the event, airframes which had already been started as the improved Fw 190A-8 fighter, were redesignated as Fw 190A-7s, the A-8 designation being reserved for a more technically upgraded machine. As such, only 80 Fw 190A-7s were produced, starting in December of 1943, before the fully developed A-8 superseded it.

Physically, the Fw 190A-7 was essentially similiar to the Fw 190A-6, but the 7.92mm fuselage MG 17 machine guns were now replaced with the larger caliber 13mm MG 131 machine guns, offering a superior rate of fire and a loading of up to 400 rounds per gun. To accommodate the larger guns, the early flat-topped fuselage armament panel was replaced with a double bulged panel. In detail, the pilot's Revi C12/D gunsight was replaced with the improved Revi 16B. Engine cowling latches were revised, while radio equipment options of the FuG 16Z and FuG 25 IFF were retained. The wing armament of four Mauser MG 151/20E cannons remained unchanged, although some machines again had the outer wing weapons deleted to suit operational needs. As before, a ventral fuselage ETC 501 rack could be added (or the simplified 300 liter tank rack) for carrying fuel or bomb loads. Also, most of the Fw 190A-7s were produced without inboard undercarriage doors, which now became the accepted practice.

Several *Rüstsätze* were planned for the Fw 190A-7, although little use would be made of them:

Rüstsätze 1 (R1) Two underwing WB 151 weapons containers, each with two MG 151 can-

Although this Fw 190A-6 has had its outer MG 151 cannons removed, the smaller fairing with its spent casing chute is visible on the underwing armament panel which replaced the bulged panel of the MG FF cannons. Also visible is the small hook indicating that this aircraft is an Fw 190A-6/R6, capable of mounting *WGr.*21 rocket tubes.

Essentially similar to the A-6, the Fw 190A-7 was the first variant to feature fuselage-mounted 13mm MG 131 machine guns, resulting in a double-bulged armament panel. White 5, an Fw 190A-7, has had its outer wing cannons removed; it appears to have flash suppressors fitted to the cowling guns. The FuG 16ZY D/F loop aerial under the aft fuselage was common from late Fw 190A-5s onward.

nons, with 145 rounds per gun. The outer wing cannons were deleted.

***Rüstsätze* 2 (R2)** The outer wing MG 151 cannons replaced with short-barreled 30mm MK 108 cannons with 55 rounds per gun.

***Rüstsätze* 3 (R3)** One 30mm MK 103 cannon under each wing with 35 rounds per gun.

***Rüstsätze* 6 (R6)** One *WGr.* 21 tube launched anti-bomber rocket beneath each wing. *Rüstsätze* 2 and 6 saw the greatest chance of operational use on the Fw 190A-7.

Doppelreiter Fuel Tanks Although many sources have stated that an Fw 190A-8 was used for the testing of extended range *Doppelreiter* (double rider) 270 liter overwing fuel tanks, more recent sources have claimed the test bed to have actually been an Fw 190A-7 (WNr. 380394). This was one of several 'slipper' tank arrangements, designed by FGZ of Stuttgart, which failed to see operational service.

Fw 190A-7s began joining combat units in early 1944, most being sent to the Western Front for Germany's defense against a seemingly endless horde of Allied bombers. In this capacity, some A-7s managed to survive until war's end, despite the horrific attrition which was soon to be suffered by the Luftwaffe.

Fuselage MG Development

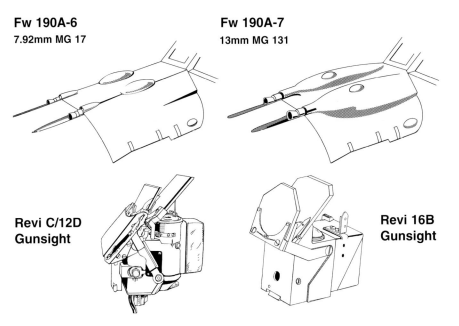

Fw 190A-6
7.92mm MG 17

Fw 190A-7
13mm MG 131

Revi C/12D Gunsight

Revi 16B Gunsight

Although only 80 Fw 190A-7s were produced, this damaged example survived until the war's end, being captured at Pilsen, Bohemia in 1945. From this viewpoint, an outstanding feature separating the A-7 from the earlier A-6 can be seen, the bulged MG 131 cover. Additionally. Fw 190A-7s retained the earlier mid-mounted pitot tube.

Late in the war, several aircraft were rigged for testing a variety of long-range 'slipper' fuel tanks designed by FGZ at Stuttgart. This Fw 190A (WNr. 380394) is equipped with 270 liter *Doppelreiter* (double rider) overwing tanks. Many sources maintain that this aircraft was an Fw 190A-8, but recent references claim it was actually an A-7. (VFW-Fokker)

FW 190A-8

As the war entered its final stages, the Fw 190A-8 became the most important of the A series variants, constituting most of the remaining numbers of Fw 190 production right to the end of hostilities. Externally, the A-8 was essentially similar to the Fw 190A-7, but with a host of refinements.

Internally, the compartment behind the pilot's cockpit now contained an additional 115 liter (30.3 gallon) fuel cell, which could be substituted with supply tanks for an MW 50 methanol-water or GM-1 nitrous-oxide engine boosting system. The tri-spherical oxygen containers were repositioned, as were the fuel lines and radio equipment. Externally, this resulted in the addition of a ventral circular access panel, an additional port side fuselage refueling cap just under the aft canopy shelf, a fuel system primer access just below the port side cockpit area, and an additional rectangular access panel just below the starboard fuselage canopy shelf.

Externally, the ventral fuselage ETC 501 rack was moved forward 20cm (eight inches) to relocate the center of gravity. Deletion of the inboard undercarriage doors was standardized. The starboard wing pitot tube was moved from the mid-point of the wing leading edge to the wing tip. Standard radio equipment consisted of FuG 16ZY and FuG 25a IFF, detectable by a ventral port wing root morane mast and aft ventral fuselage D/F loop (FuG 16ZY) and the aft ventral whip aerial (FuG 25a).

Armament remained unchanged with two fuselage mounted MG 131 machine guns (400 rounds per gun), wing root MG 151/20E cannons (250 rounds per gun) and two outboard MG 151/20E cannons (125 rounds per gun). Slightly raised rectangular plates were added to the wing's upper surfaces in conjunction with the outboard MG 151 cannons. When carried, a gun camera (EK 16 or BSK 16) was mounted on an inboard position of the port wing leading edge.

For additional equipment the Fw 190A-8 relied almost entirely on *Rüstsätzen*:

Rüstsätze 1 (R1) A WB 151 weapons container under each wing, each containing two 20mm MG 151/20E cannons with 125 rounds per gun.

Rüstsätze 2 (R2) Two 30mm MK 108 cannons with 55 rounds per gun, replacing the outboard wing MG 151 cannons.

Rüstsätze 3 (R3) A pod-mounted 30mm MK 103 cannon beneath each wing for anti-bomber or ground-attack use. An improved design of the coverings featured a hinged center section for cannon breech access and tapered coverings over the long cannon barrels. This *Rüstsätze* saw limited operational use, if any, due to its detrimental weight and drag.

Rüstsätzen 4 and **5 (R4** and **R5)** According to some, these kits respectively indicated the installation of an engine boosting system (such as the GM-1) or the additional 115 liter (30.3 gallon) fuel cell in the aft fuselage. While other sources claim the R4 designation referred to an equipment pack for the outboard MG 151 20mm cannons.

Rüstsätze 6 (R6) One tube-launched *WGr.* 21 (21cm) anti-bomber rocket mounted beneath each wing. So effective had these weapons proven to be, that the RLM specified that fifty per cent of Fw 190A-8s produced be capable of mounting the R6 conversion off the assembly lines.

Rüstsätze 7 (R7) *Sturmjäger* (assault fighter) with additional internal and external armor plating for anti-bomber operations. This consisted of internal armor for the fuselage MG 131 bay (4mm lower and 15mm rear), external side fuselage plates (5mm), side canopy and windshield quarterpanel armored glass (30mm) and forward windshield (50mm).

Rüstsätze 8 (R8) A combination of R2 (outboard 30mm MK 108 cannons) and R7 *Sturmjäger* armor plating. This additionally allowed for the protection of the outboard Mk 108 cannons and ammunition bins with 4mm internal wing armored plates. This *Rüstsätze* was particularly popular with dedicated *Rammjäger* anti-bomber defense *Staffeln* and *Gruppen* operating on the Western Front.

Rüstsätze 11 (R11) An all weather fighter conversion, equipped with a BMW 801TU or TS powerplant, FuG 16ZE and FuG 125 radio gear, a PKS 12 auto-pilot system, and a heated windshield.

Rüstsätze 12 (R12) A combination of R2 (MK 108 outboard cannons) and R11 (all-weather fighter equipment), but with a standard BMW 801D-2 engine.

Beyond the use of conversion sets, other versions of the Fw 190A-8 were created for specialized missions. The Fw 190A-8 *Nacht Jabo-Rei* (Night Long-range Fighter-bomber) featured fluted exhaust dampers, underwing 300 liter fuel tanks on Messerschmitt designed wing racks, and the removal of the outboard wing cannons. The Fw 190A-8 could serve as a *Jabo* by carrying a bomb load on its ventral ETC 501 rack and having its outboard wing cannons deleted. With the removal of the outer cannons the underwing armament panel could be

Red 22 was one of many Fw 190A-8's found derelict by the victorious Allies. The small hole below the soldier's arm is the primer access for the fuel system and the small triangle marking just below the rear cockpit shelf marks a fuel cap for the aft fuselage 115 liter internal tank fitted to A-8's. The aircraft was equipped with an FuG 16ZY morane antenna, an FuG 16ZY D/F loop aerial and an FuG 25 IFF antenna. The red and yellow Defense of the Reich fuselage bands denote JG 301. (Gene Stafford)

Wing Development

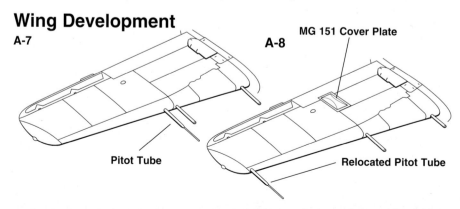

A-7

A-8

MG 151 Cover Plate

Pitot Tube

Relocated Pitot Tube

replaced with a smooth access plate, eliminating the faired spent casing chutes, and in this form the Fw 190A-8 *Jabo* became indistinguishable from the Fw 190F-8 ground-assault variant.

As the borders of the Third Reich continued to shrink, the Fw 190 *Jagdgruppen* were pressed into bitter combats on a daily basis. Along with interceptor and *Jabo* missions, the head on, near suicidal attacks of the *Rammjäger* pilots bespoke of the desperate courage of the Luftwaffe during the Reich's dying months. Earlier variants of the Fw 190 were fitted with *Sturmjäger* armor to increase their survivability (such as the remaining A-6s and A-7s), while still other Fw 190s had their armament stripped to just the wing root 20mm cannons for greater speed. Unusual variations of weapons were experimented with, such as a single rear firing ventral fuselage *WGr.* 21 rocket tube, which allowed a projectile to be discharged into a bomber formation following a *Sturmböcken* (battering ram) attack. In short, anything which would bring down an Allied bomber was considered crucial to Germany's existence. The aerial conflict on the Eastern Front and in the Mediterranean was equally tenacious.

Production of the Fw 190A-8 was terminated only by the factories being overrun during the spring of 1945. While Fw 190s had been churned out of underground assembly lines "like hot rolls", lack of fuel and experienced pilots had rendered the production effort almost useless. Kurt Tank's astounding fighter littered airfields around Europe along with the broken remains of other Luftwaffe machines.

After the war, some of the Fw 190s produced by SNCA for France under the designation NC 900 were built partially to Fw 190A-8 standards, with MG 131 fuselage armament cowlings. One of these survives today at the *Musee de l'Air du Bourget*, near Paris. Fittingly, it wears the markings of an Fw 190A-8 flown by *Oberstleutnant* Josef 'Pips' Priller at the time of the June 1944 Allied invasion of France. One of Germany's most colorful planes, representing one of her most heroic pilots.

The Fw 190A-8 possessed several detailed refinements over the A-7. Behind the open fuel cap is an additional starboard access panel. The upper wing surface featured rectangular raised access plates for the outboard MG 151 cannons (visible above the undercarriage leg).

Detail Development

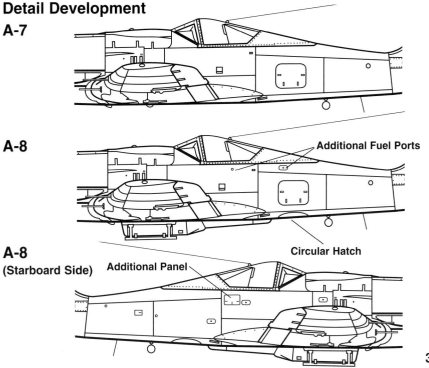

A-7

A-8

Additional Fuel Ports

A-8 (Starboard Side)

Additional Panel

Circular Hatch

FW 190A-9

The Fw 190A-9 designation was proposed as a high altitude, high performance version of the Fw 190A-8. Externally similar to the A-8, the A-9 was to be equipped with a BMW 801F-1 engine, provisionally driving broad chord propeller blades. Due to problems with the BMW 801F, only two *Versuch* aircraft received this powerplant (the Fw 190V-35 and V-36); subsequent airframes were equipped with 2,200 hp BMW 801TS/TH engines.

Armament was the same as the Fw 190A-8, including the fuselage ETC 501 rack, normally utilizing a 300 liter fuel tank. One external innovation was the installation of a 'blown hood' canopy offering greater visibility for the pilot, the armored headrest now being supported by a fully tapered pylon. This canopy would be retro-fitted to a number of Fw 190A-8s and would be factory installed on late war Fw 190F ground-attack variants. A limited number of *Rüstsätzen* were planned for the Fw 190A-9, these being R2, R11 and R12 (with the same designated equipment as the A-8).

FW 190A-10

The Fw 190A-10 was to be a ground-attack version of the A-9 with wing mounted MK 103 30mm cannons, enlarged main wheels and a BMW 801TS/TH powerplant. Several weapons packages were planned for the A-10, which was to be produced by recycling older Fw 190 airframes, rather than establishing a dedicated assembly line. As the war situation worsened, the Fw 190A-10 was cancelled.

Bomb Rack

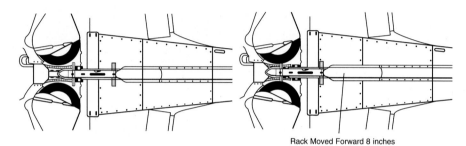

Rack Moved Forward 8 inches

Fw 190A-7   Fw 190A-8

Like earlier variants, the Fw 190A-8 could be converted to a *Jabo* with the outer wing cannons removed and a centerline bomb load on the ETC 501 rack. In this configuration it would be identical to its armored ground assault counterpart, the Fw 190F-8. The wing tip pitot tube was introduced on the A-8 series.

The *RLM* dictated that 50 percent of the Fw 190A-8s production should be capable of carrying *Rüstsätze* 6. Armorers of JG 26 slide a 21cm (210mm) *WGr.* 21 rocket into the launch tube. The main support hook and electrical triggering connections are visible.

After the rocket was loaded, the support rods were tightened. The tubes were angled upward, allowing the pilot to gauge optimum attacking position and trajectory. The pitot tube which was installed on the starboard wing was moved to an outboard position on the Fw 190A-8.

Finalized Rüstsätzen

R1

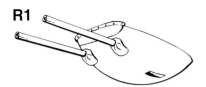

Fw 190A-5/U11, A-6/R1, A-7/R1, A-8/R1

R2

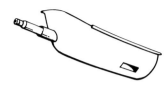

External 30mm Mk 108 (Experimental)

R2 and R8

Fw 190A-6, A-7, A-8 (Internal Mk108)

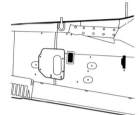

Mk 108 Wing Underside

R3

30mm Mk 103 Cannon

R3 (Late)

Extended Pod

Vertical Fluting

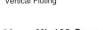

30mm Mk 103 Cannon

R6

WGr 21 Aerial Rocket

R8 Internal Armor for Mk 108 Cannon

R7 and R8

Fw 190A-8 (WNr. 681382) was converted to a full A-8/R8 *Rammjäger* (ram fighter). The R8 conversion was a combination of *Rüstsätze* 2 (outer wing MK 108 30mm cannons) and *Rüstsätze* 7 (additional fuselage and canopy armor). The fuselage side armor was 5mm thick and the armored glass canopy side panels were 30mm thick.

Rammjägers assigned to specialized *Sturmstaffeln* often carried unique markings. This black cowled Fw 190A-8/R8 was reportedly flown by Willie Maximowitz of 11.(*Sturm*)/*JG* 3. The shorter barrels of the outboard 30mm MK 108 cannons can be seen, as well as the 30mm armored glass panels of the side windshield.

30mm Armor

50mm Armor

5mm Armor

Some Fw 190A-8s were converted in the field to variants for which there were no designations. These aircraft have been fitted with underwing 300 liter fuel tanks (on Messerschmitt carriers) and 'fluted' exhaust dampers to serve as *Nacht Jabo-Rei* nocturnal intruders serving with *NSGr* 20 in 1944

Cowling panels could be removed entirely, rendering the BMW 801 powerplant totally accessible for maintenance. The inboard position gun camera was common from the Fw 190A-6 thru A-8 variants, as well as the Fw 190F-8 and G-8 series.

Fw 190A-8 Nacht Jabo-Rei

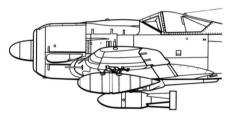

Fluted Exhaust Flame Dampers

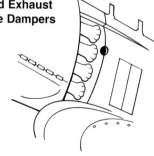

Drop Tank Variations

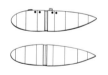

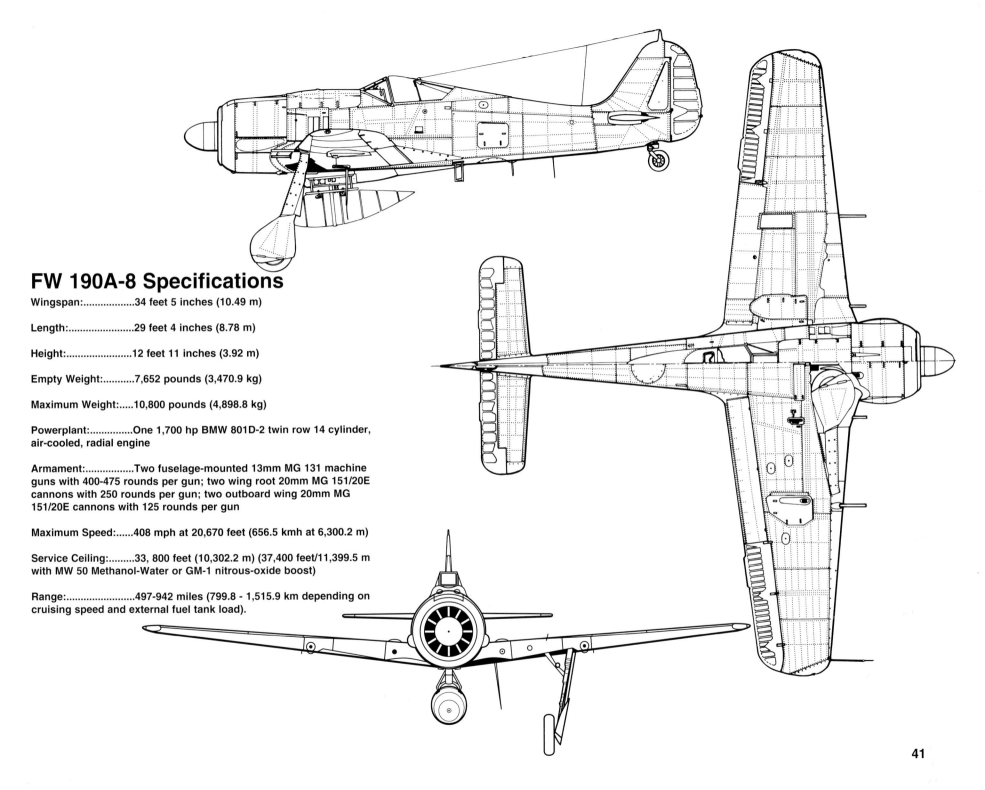

FW 190A-8 Specifications

Wingspan:................34 feet 5 inches (10.49 m)

Length:.....................29 feet 4 inches (8.78 m)

Height:.....................12 feet 11 inches (3.92 m)

Empty Weight:...........7,652 pounds (3,470.9 kg)

Maximum Weight:.....10,800 pounds (4,898.8 kg)

Powerplant:...............One 1,700 hp BMW 801D-2 twin row 14 cylinder, air-cooled, radial engine

Armament:.................Two fuselage-mounted 13mm MG 131 machine guns with 400-475 rounds per gun; two wing root 20mm MG 151/20E cannons with 250 rounds per gun; two outboard wing 20mm MG 151/20E cannons with 125 rounds per gun

Maximum Speed:......408 mph at 20,670 feet (656.5 kmh at 6,300.2 m)

Service Ceiling:.........33, 800 feet (10,302.2 m) (37,400 feet/11,399.5 m with MW 50 Methanol-Water or GM-1 nitrous-oxide boost)

Range:.......................497-942 miles (799.8 - 1,515.9 km depending on cruising speed and external fuel tank load).

FW 190 Nachtjäger

By late 1943 single engined fighters were being accepted into specialized units of the *Nachtjagdverbände,* especially those using *Wilde Sau* (Wild Boar) tactics to help defend against the fleets of RAF bombers. In effect, these fighters were sent up to attack British bombers using whatever visual contact could be made by the glare of searchlights, flares, or burning targets. The two principal single engine fighters that would participate in this struggle: the Messerschmitt Bf 109 and the Focke-Wulf Fw 190.

As on-board search radars became available in quantity, *Nachtjäger* conversions were made to Fw 190A-6 and A-8 variants, using FuG 216 (*Neptun* V) and FuG 217 (*Neptun* J-2 and J-3) devices. On both the A-6 and A-5 versions, exhaust shields could be added below the fuselage armament panel; flash suppressors were optional on the fuselage machine guns, and landing lights could be installed in the leading edge of the outer port wing. The fuselage ETC 801 rack was often retained for carrying a 300 liter fuel tank, extending the Fw 190's combat duration. The *Rüstsätze* 11 (R11) conversion set could also be utilized, providing the Fw 190 *Nachtjäger* with all-weather capability.

Externally, two principal radar antenna arrays were utilized, consisting of whip aerials (Yagi type antennas) along the fuselage spine and outer wing panels (up to twenty plus elements), or a system of two support masts on the leading edge of each wing with each mast carrying two dipole elements. Most sources confirm that the Fw 190A-6 *Nachtjäger* was normally fitted with the whip aerial arrangement, whereas the Fw 190A-8 was seen with either installation. The pilot's radar indicator was usually installed in the upper left hand area of the cockpit instrument panel.

Fw 190s participating in *Wilde Sau* missions were not always radar equipped variants. Some units employed straight fighters or *nachtjabo* (night fighter-bombers) if needed. Single engined *Wilde Sau* aircraft were employed less and less into 1944 as twin engined radar equipped aircraft again assumed control of night defense duties. Still, some units were reorganized specif-

NachtJäger Radar (Neptun J-3) and Accessories

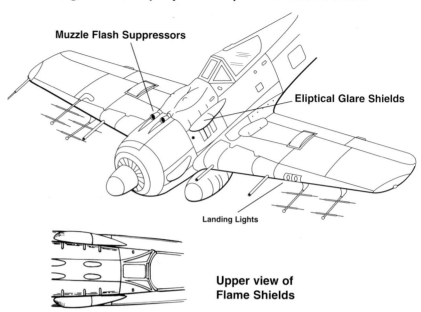

Muzzle Flash Suppressors

Eliptical Glare Shields

Landing Lights

Upper view of Flame Shields

ically for the purpose of combating marauding British Mosquito nightfighters, extending the use of the single engined *Nachtjäger*. Fighter *Staffeln* and specialized *Gruppen* using the Fw 190A for nocturnal missions included *NJG* 11, *NJG*r 10 and *SKG* 10.

Fw 190A-6

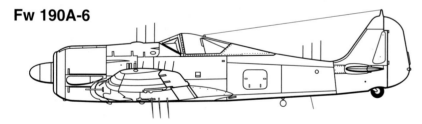

Fw 190A-8

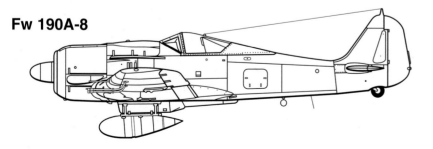

White 11 was an Fw 190A-6 *Nachtjäger* (night fighter) flown by *Oberleutnant* Krause of 1./*NJGr* 10 in 1944. It was equipped with FuG 217 *Neptun* radar, anti glare shields and flash suppressors on its fuselage guns. Variations of the stylized *Wilde Sau* (Wild Boar) emblem were carried by Fw 190s serving in the night-interceptor role.

FW 190F Jabo

Once it was realized that the Fw 190A performed exceedingly well in the ground-attack role by late 1942, it was decided to create a dedicated series of close support machines under the designation Fw 190F. This plan was further promoted by the fact that Germany's main ground attack weapon, the two-seat Junkers Ju 87 *Stuka*, was obsolete, while the single-seat Fw 190 could deliver similar payloads with far greater speed and efficiency.

A common trait of all Fw 190Fs was the elimination of the outboard wing cannons, restricting armament to the fuselage machine guns and wing root MG 151 cannons. As with many of the earlier Fw 190A *Jabo* conversions, the underwing hinged armament panels (bulged or with spent casing outlets) were replaced by a flat panel.

For survivability in low level operations, Fw 190Fs were protected with additional internal armor plating around critical areas: the lower engine (6mm), lower fuselage (5mm) and the aft fuselage fuel cells (8mm). This armor, together with the already standard cowling ring armor (5.5mm and 6.5mm) and the pilot's cockpit armor (12-14mm headrest, 8mm seat back and 5mm aft plating) made for a sturdy, dependable machine. Overall performance was inhibited by these progressive modifications, however, resulting in the Fw 190F-8 (one of the last variants produced) having an average speed of 520 km/h (322.4 mph) and a range of 775 kilometers (480.4 miles) at a loaded weight of 5,400 kg (11,905 pounds).

Although some have insisted that all early Fw 190Fs (F-1, F-2 and F-3) were manufactured with tropical cowling intakes as standard, evidence exists to indicate that these intakes were supplied as a uniform option to be fitted as needed and removed if necessary. In the event, Fw 190F variants were often externally identical to the Fw 190A *Jabo* conversions which had preceded them.

Fw 190F-1

The Fw 190F-1 was produced in very limited numbers, only about thirty machines, and was based on the Fw 190A-4/U3 *Jabo* factory conversion, with its ventral fuselage ETC-501 rack and outboard cannons removed. As well as the usual stores that could be carried, the F-1 also made use of the *Einhängerost* 4 (ER 4) multiple bomb carrying pallet which normally held four 50kg (110lb) SC 50 bombs. Radio equipment consisted of FuG 16Z and FuG 25 IFF, although radio gear not considered necessary on the Eastern Front (where most F-1s served) was often removed. Production of the Fw 190F-1 was terminated in mid 1943.

Fw 190F Internal Armor

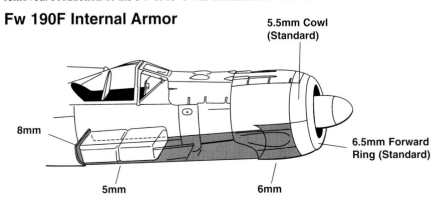

5.5mm Cowl (Standard)

6.5mm Forward Ring (Standard)

8mm

5mm

6mm

The Fw 190F-1 was based on the Fw 190A-4/U3 *Jabo* conversion and built in limited numbers. Without tropical cowling intakes (which some sources claim was standard on the F-1, F-2 and F-3 models) the F-1 was externally identical to the A-4/U3. Most were assigned to the Eastern Front.

The Fw 190F-2 was the armored close support version of the Fw 190A-5/U3, with the two variants being nearly identical and easily confused. Both the Fw 190A *Jabos* and Fw 190Fs could be equipped with the ER 4 (*Einhängerost* 4) multiple bomb rack, which mounted four SC 50 (110 lb) bombs.

FW 190F-2

The Fw 190F-2 was based on the Fw 190A-5/U3 factory conversion, being externally identical to the A-5 model with its six-inch extension of the forward fuselage. Similar to the F-1 the defensive armament was reduced to the fuselage mounted MG 17 machine guns and the wing root MG 151 cannons. Bomb load capacity was the same, utilizing the fuselage ETC 501 rack. Many Fw 190F-2s were produced with side-cowling air intakes with tropical filters. Production ceased after 270 F-2s had been delivered, most of them to the Eastern Front, although a number were used in the Mediterranean theater.

FW 190F-3

Production of the Fw 190F-3 was based on the Fw 190A-5/U17 factory conversion, which allowed for greater bomb load capacity. With the majority of F-3s being F-3/R1s, four additional ETC 50 bomb racks were fitted beneath the outboard wings, within streamlined fairings, for carrying four 50 kg (110 lb) bombs. On many Fw 190F-3s, tropical cowling intakes were added and an optional gun camera could be installed in the wing leading edge. Plans were made for the availability of the *Rüstsätze* 3 conversion set of two 30mm MK 103 underwing cannons for anti-tank operations, but this saw little, if any, use.

Just over 270 Fw 190F-3s were produced at the Arado facility before the series was terminated — most examples were sent to the Eastern Front. Production of the Fw 190F series was suspended by the introduction of the Fw 190G. The Fw 190F-4, F-5 and F-6 were ultimately cancelled. However, production of the Fw 190F series was re-established with the introduction of the Fw 190F-8 in 1944.

Fw 190F-3s were adapted from the Fw 190A-5/U3 and Fw 190A-5/U17 with underwing bomb racks. Four underwing ETC 50 racks were installed with the *Rüstsätze* 1 conversion for the F-3. These Eastern Front machines are also equipped with sand filters, making them Fw 190F-3/R1/Trops by full designation.

The ETC 50 underwing racks of the Fw 190F-3 featured streamlined housings, and both the racks and housings were finished in the Light Blue underside color. On earlier variant Fw 190As, up to the A-5 and the F-1 through F-3, the gun camera was positioned in the outboard wing, accessible via a hinged cover.

A ground crew prepares to load this Fw 190F-3/R1/Trop with an AB 250 (*Abwurfbehalter* - droppable container) which opened along its sides to dispense smaller bomblets or anti-personnel grenades. Rear details of the ETC 50 racks are visible.

FW 190F-8

In 1944 the Fw 190F-8 began rolling off the assembly lines, serving as the ground-attack counterpart to the Fw 190A-8 fighter. In virtually all detailed respects, it was identical to the A-8, but with its outboard cannons removed and fitted with an ETC 501 fuselage rack as standard. The fuselage MG 131 machine guns were retained under a bulged armament panel, as well as the wing root MG 151 cannons. On some F-8s, the upper wing rectangular plates associated with the deleted outboard wing cannons were eliminated and similar to the A-8, the pitot tube was moved to the wing tip. The F-8 also had the option of carrying an extra aft-fuselage 115 liter internal fuel tank. The Fw 190F-8 also featured the newly approved *Grosse Bombelektrik* weapons-control system which allowed the pilot to select the release of his weapons stores or opt for a full salvo during attacks.

On late model Fw 190F-8s, the improved 'blown hood' canopy with a pylon mounted headrest was made available for improved pilot vision. This canopy was retro-fitted to Fw 190A-8 fighters when available. Radio equipment options and internal upgrades of the F-8 were the same as the A-8.

Several *Rüstsätzen* were planned for the Fw 190F-8, as well as an impressive number of armament test beds. Some of the more notable were as follows:

***Rüstsätze* 1 (R1)** allowed for the addition of four ETC 50 underwing bomb racks for four SC 50 (110lb) bombs. This was the most popular conversion set, seeing widespread use. Late in the war the ETC 50 racks were at times supplanted by the smaller ETC 71 racks carrying a similar weapons load.

***Rüstsätze* 3 (R3)** allowed for the installation of two underwing 30mm MK 103 cannons with improved, tapered external pods. By this time, however, research with the MK 103 cannon pods was being terminated and it is believed that only two F-8s were so equipped.

***Rüstsätze* 13 (R13)** was a nocturnal attack version equipped with all-weather apparatus.

WGr. 28/32 Rockets were based on the unguided infantry rockets, these 280mm and 320mm blunt nosed projectiles were tested as underwing mounts against ground targets with little success.

Panzerschreck (Tank Terror) long triple tube underwing launchers for 88mm anti-armor projectiles. Although unsuccessful, this was one of several similar arrangements tested with alternate caliber weapons under different designations.

SG 113 *Förstersonde* was two aerofoil, vertical pylons passing through the inboard wings, allowing for the downward firing of 75mm anti-armor projectiles (two tubes in each pylon). This arrangement was similiar in principal to the fuselage mounted, upward firing, triple tube **SG 116 *Zellendusche*** anti-bomber weapon tested for Fw 190A-8 fighters. Both weapons were triggered by a sensor which detected passing targets.

X-4 *Ruhrstahl* Rockets reportedly, several Fw 190F-8s were rigged for tests with these underwing, wire-guided, air-to-air rockets in late 1944 and early 1945. The rockets, mounted one per wing on ETC 503 racks, produced interesting results, but were not used operationally.

Panzerblitz (Tank Lightning) inspired by *Panzerschreck*, these modified R4M air-to-air rockets were mounted under the outboard wings on flat launching pallets. *Panzerblitz* 1 (Pb 1) featured fixed fin 80mm projectiles requiring extended launch rails, whereas *Panzerblitz* 2 (Pb 2) featured folding fin rockets on more compact pallets. Six to seven of these weapons could be carried under each wing for anti-armor operations. The Fw 190F-8 and F-9 used them operationally beginning in early 1945.

Bv 246 *Hagelkorn* (Hailstone) A single Fw 190F-8 was modified to carry the Blohm und

The Fw 190F-8 was the armored close support version of the Fw 190A-8 fighter, which was also identifiable by its bulged gun cowl for two 13mm MG 131 machine guns. This aircraft is believed to be the prototype of the F-8 series, complete with tropical filters and four underwing ETC 50 racks.

An SC 250 (551 lb) bomb is wheeled into position beneath an Fw 190F-8's ETC 501 centerline rack. Slits of light above the rack and its fuselage fairing confirm that these attachments were anything but flush fitting! The yellow stripes on the bomb indicate a high explosive weapon.

Voss Bv 246 glide bomb. The body of the weapon was attached to the fuselage ETC 501 ventral rack with its wings spanning beneath the wings of the Fw 190. Stabilizing rods pushed the wings of the Bv 246 downward at the tips to spring it away from the underside of the Fw 190 upon release.

Until the end of the war, Fw 190F-8s were being encountered by advancing Allied forces on all fronts. Fw 190Fs served alongside the Fw 190A *Jabos* of various *Schlachtgeschwaders,* most notably *SG* 1, 2, and 4. *SG* 2 (previously *Stukageschwader* 2) was the home unit of Germany's highly decorated hero, *Oberst* Hans Ulrich Rudel, who split his combat sorties between his beloved Ju 87G tank busting *Stuka* and his Fw 190

Although Germany's allies were not supplied with the Fw 190 on a large-scale basis, some 70 Fw 190F-8s were dispatched to Hungarian Air Force units for use as fighter bombers in late 1944 and early 1945. Prior to the anti-Axis coup in August of 1944, a limited number of Fw 190s were also used by Rumanian air units.

Wing Details

Fw 190F-1, F-2, F-3

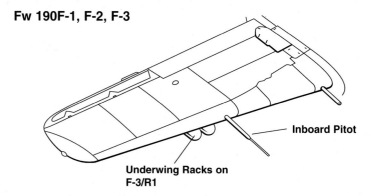

Inboard Pitot

Underwing Racks on F-3/R1

Fw 190F-8

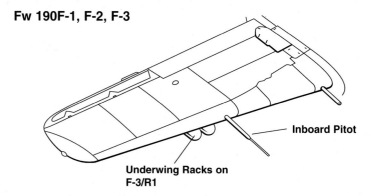

Upper MG 151 Cover Plate Removed on some F-8s

Underwing Racks on F-8/R1

Outboard Pitot

Like the Fw 190A-8, the F-8 could be identified by its wing tip pitot tube. Without underwing racks the F-8 was externally the same as an A-8 converted to the *Jabo* role. These F-8s of an Eastern Front *Schlachtgeschwader* display simple markings and have been stripped of their auxiliary radio gear (FuG 25, FuG 16ZY), which was less needed on the Russian Front.

I *Gruppe/SG* 4 was one of the best documented units serving in Italy during 1944. At one time all of their Fw 190F-8s featured a common desert camouflage and white spirals on their propeller spinners. Most were F-8s without underwing ETC 50 racks.

Some Fw 190F-8s did not feature the rectangular MG 151 upper wing access panel normally found on the Fw 190A-8. The F-8s of SG 4 appear to lack this feature. The unit emblem was an axe wielding Mickey Mouse riding a green bomb on a white circle.

The Fw 190F-8 received the designation Fw 190F-8/R1 when equipped with under wing ETC 50 bomb racks. Later models were also fitted with 'blown hoods' with a pylon supported headrest. These winter camouflaged F-8s of *Schlachtgeschwader* 2 have had their lower undercarriage doors removed to prevent snow and mud from clogging around the wheels. (Hans Obert)

Canopy Development Fw 190F-8

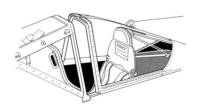

Standard **Late Model Blown Canopy**

Underwing Bomb Racks

Outboard Camera F-2 and F-3

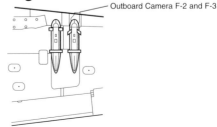

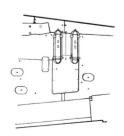

ETC 50 (F-3/R1 and F-8/R1) **ETC 71 (Late F-8)**

Both the Fw 190A-8 and F-8 could be equipped with optional 30mm MK 103 cannons under the R3 conversion. These were an improvement over the earlier *Rüstsätze* 3, now with tapered fairings over the cannon barrels and vertical muzzle fluting. In the event, the F-8/R3 saw only limited use — reportedly only two were built.

47

Aircraft of II *Gruppe/SG* 4 serving on the Russian Front featured extensive yellow theater markings. Black E is an Fw 190F-8 carrying an AB 250 weapons container, but no underwing racks. Other machines in this unit were F-8/R1s and some displayed simplified variations of the colorful unit trim.

Near the end of the war, ground-attack units sported yellow nose and tail trim for identification. Yellow cowling bands and rudders were a popular variation. This F-8/R1 also had simplified outline-style crosses. (Richard F. Grant)

Fw 190F Family

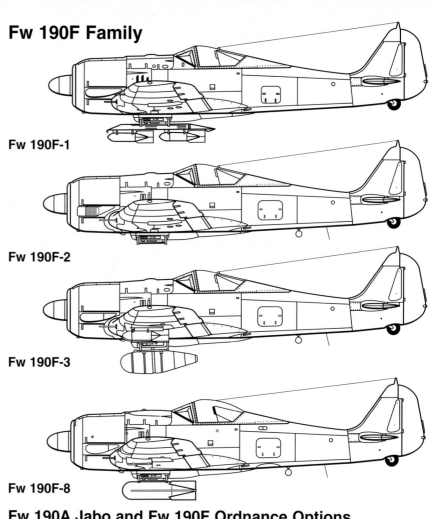

Fw 190F-1

Fw 190F-2

Fw 190F-3

Fw 190F-8

Fw 190A Jabo and Fw 190F Ordnance Options

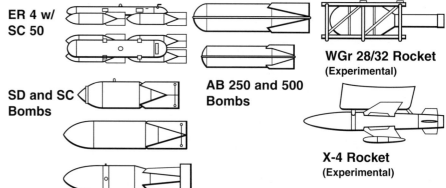

ER 4 w/ SC 50

SD and SC Bombs

AB 250 and 500 Bombs

WGr 28/32 Rocket
(Experimental)

X-4 Rocket
(Experimental)

Although little has been documented regarding Rumanian use of the Fw 190, some were utilized by the *Aeronautica Regal Romana* (Royal Rumanian Aeronautics) before Rumania's anti-Axis rebellion during the late summer of 1944. German markings have been crudely replaced with the yellow, blue and red Rumanian crosses and rudder stripes.

The Hungarian Air Force received some 70 Fw 190F-8s. These late examples retained German markings with most having large white cowl numbers. The pilot of the 102 Fighter-Bomber Group has his nick name "Bumerang" painted under the windshield. (Horvath via Stapfer)

FW 190F-9

Externally similar to the Fw 190F-8, the F-9 differed in having a 2,200 hp BMW 801TS (turbo-supercharged) powerplant, driving broader chord wooden VDM 9-12157H3 propellers. Most F-9s featured the new 'blown hood' canopy and *Rüstsätze* sets were provided under much the same designations as those of the Fw 190F-8. Like the F-8, the F-9 was optionally equipped with the smaller ETC 71 underwing bomb racks and *Panzerblitz* rockets near the war's end.

Fw 190F-9s served in mixed units with F-8s on both the Western and Eastern Fronts in limited numbers. Reportedly, a few F-9s were converted to torpedo carriers for use by the special operations unit III *Gruppe/KG* 200 during the early spring of 1945, but such use was extremely limited. Further versions of the Fw 190F were planned beyond the F-9, but other than those machines manufactured as test aircraft, these variants did not see production.

The Fw 190F-9 was powered by a 2,200 hp BMW 801TS engine driving broad chord VDM propeller blades. This aircraft of an unknown ground attack unit also carried *Panzerblitz* rockets beneath its wings. The launch pallets were often finished in a dark color, either dark gray or black. (Meixner)

Panzerblitz Rockets (Fw 190F-8 and Fw 190F-9)

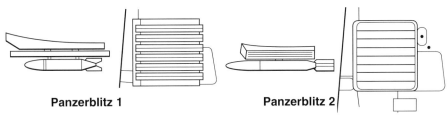

Panzerblitz 1   Panzerblitz 2

FW 190G-1

The Fw 190G variant was conceived as a dedicated high speed, long-range fighter-bomber (*Jagdbomber-Reichweite* or *Jabo-Rei*). The first of these, the Fw 190G-1, was based directly on the Fw 190A-4/U8 conversion, with 300 liter underwing fuel tanks suspended on Junkers type faired mountings, and a fuselage ETC 501 rack for a bomb load. To reduce weight for extra speed and range, defensive armament was reduced to only the 20mm wing root MG 151 cannons. In fact, the elimination of the fuselage and outer wing guns was a trait of all subsequent Fw 190G variants.

Only 49 Fw 190G-1s, based on the A-4 airframe, are believed to have been produced before manufacturing centers converted to the extended fuselages (Fw 190A-5s and subsequent airframes). By 1943, surviving examples of the original Fw 190A-4/U8 conversions were reportedly redesignated as Fw 190G-1s.

Fw 190G-1 (Fw 190A-4/U8)

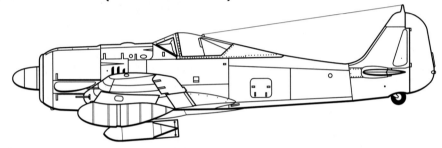

FW 190G-2

The Fw 190G-2 was based on the extended nose Fw 190A-5/U2, U8, and U13 factory conversions, all of which had been designed as *Jabo-Rei* variants. Armament was reduced to just the wing root 20mm cannons and a fuselage ETC 501 rack for bomb loads. Underwing 300 liter fuel tanks were usually suspended on the more simplified unfaired Messerschmitt *Trägers* (Messerschmitt carriers), which were readily identifiable by their N shaped bracing struts. Although more complex in their appearance, the Messerschmitt racks produced less drag than the Junkers style faired mounts, affording greater speed.

A further limited production version was the Fw 190G-2/N (*Nacht Jabo-Rei* - night long range fighter-bomber), which was equipped with 'fluted' flame damper extensions on the exhaust pipes. An additional detail of Fw 190G-2s operating in either the day or night role, was the optional installation of a gun camera in the outer port wing.

Sources differ on the number of Fw 190G-2s produced; some indicate as few as 468, while later estimates claim over 600 machines had rolled off assembly lines. Fw 190G-2s were pressed into service on all fronts with *Schlachtgeschwaders* and specialized bombing *Staffeln* within *Jagdgeschwaders*. Some were issued to *Kampfgeschwaders* (bomber units) while still others were assigned to *NachtschlachtGruppen* (night ground-attack groups).

Factory fresh Fw 190G-2s prepare to run up their engines during acceptance testing. Some G-2s were delivered without underwing racks for fuel tanks, but were typical in having the fuselage guns removed. The blast troughs in the upper cowling were either smoothed over or fitted with tapered fairings.

These Eastern Front Fw 190s of SG 152 (an operational training unit) have variously been described as Fw 190A-5/U3s and F-2s, but the absence of fuselage guns on the machine in the foreground indicates that it is likely a G-2. The black triangle marking was common with many close support units.

FW 190G-3

The Fw 190G-3 was again based on Fw 190A-5 or A-6 airframes, entering production during the summer of 1943. Armament and load carrying capacity was the same as that of the Fw 190G-2, however, the G-3 was characterized by the installation of two Focke-Wulf designed under wing racks, referred to as Focke-Wulf *Trägers* (Focke-Wulf carriers). These carriers were distinctive in being elongated pylons with adjustable side braces. The Focke-Wulf *Trägers* were capable of carrying either two 300 liter fuel tanks (one under each wing) or two underwing bombs, the usual load being a 250 kg (551 lb) weapon, although each rack was capable of sustaining a larger load. This allowed the Fw 190G-3 the flexibility of being equipped with a fuselage bomb with underwing tanks for long range missions, a fuselage 300 liter tank with two underwing bombs for medium range missions, or a triple bomb load for short range attacks.

Some Fw 190G-3s were equipped with the PKS 11 or 12 auto-pilot system, while a further small number were tested with GM-1 nitrous-oxide engine boosting systems. Optionally, some G-3s were outfitted with tropicalized cowling intakes, while a limited number were equipped with night-bombing 'fluted' exhaust dampers and port wing landing lights under the designation Fw 190G-3/N (for *Nacht Jabo-Rei*).

Late in the war, some Fw 190G-3s were retro-fitted with four underwing ETC 50 bomb racks (two under each wing) under the designation Fw 190G-3/R1. The *Rüstsätze* 1 field conversion had been made available for the Fw 190F, allowing for the carrying of four 50 kg (110 lb) underwing bombs, and as the war situation worsened for Germany, surviving Fw 190G's were modified according to tactical needs.

Fw 190G-3s were dispatched to all war fronts, particularly Russian Front *Schlachtgeschwaders* and Mediterranean units such as *Schlachtgeschwader* 4, where some examples fell intact into Allied hands.

Precise production figures for Fw 190Gs (and later F variants) remain vague, likely due to concurrent manufacture with Fw 190A fighters and the constant recycling of earlier models. Proposals for Fw 190G-4 through G-7 variants did not produce combat replacements for the Fw 190G-3, being limited to paper projects and few actual prototypes.

Fw 190G-2

Fw 190G-3

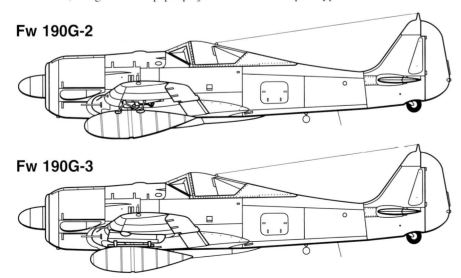

As a *Jabo-Rei*, the Fw 190G-2 was normally equipped with two 300 liter fuel tanks on low-drag Messerschmitt *Trägers* with bracing struts. The G-2 *Jabo-Rei* bore a strong resemblance to the Fw 190A-5/U2 and A-5/U8 conversions from which it was adapted.

Fitted with 'fluted' flame damper on the exhausts, the Fw 190G-2 was designated the Fw 190G-2/N *Nacht Jabo-Rei*. Sources indicate that the same modifications could be made to the Fw 190G-3 under the designation G-3/N. These machines saw action with *NSGr* 20 (*Nachtschlachtgruppe* 20) for raids against England in 1944.

The Fw 190G-3 was essentially the same as the G-2, but equipped with the improved Focke-Wulf *Trägers* beneath the wings. These racks could carry either 300 liter tanks or bombs (usually 250kg/551lb bombs).

The empty fuselage gun bay demonstrates a feature of all Fw 190Gs, the removal of the fuselage mounted machine guns. The inboard positioned pitot tube also was common to the G-1 through G-3 variants. Fw 190Gs saw combat on all fronts.

Under Wing Rack Development

Fw 190G-1 (Fw 190A-4/U8)   **Junkers Faired Racks w/ 300 Liter Tank**

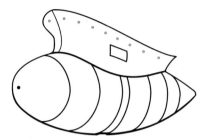

Fw 190G-2   **Messerschmitt Braced Racks w/ 300 Liter Tank**

Fw 190G-3   **Focke-Wulf Pylon Racks w/ 300 Liter Tank or Bomb Load**

Fw 190G-8   **ETC 503 Racks w/ Bomb Load or 300 Liter Tank**

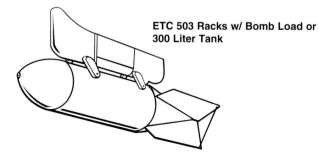

An Fw 190G-3 taxies out for a mission from its Mediterranean base. Sunlight has illuminated another feature of the Focke-Wulf carriers, the small side fairings that connected to the wing underside. What appears to be a fork like object in front of the cowling is the leg of an obstacle spotter sitting on the starboard wing.

During its initial flight evaluations over the Ohio country side by the USAAF, DN+FP retained its factory camouflage and wing national insignia, although the fuselage and tail markings do not appear to be original. The upper cowling machine gun channels were faired over, a common feature of the Fw 190G series.

DN+FP was an Fw 190G-3 captured by the Allies in the Mediterranean. Although all armament has been stripped, the locations of the underwing Focke-Wulf pylon racks are still visible. This machine was shipped to the United States for testing at Wright Field (now Wright-Patterson Air Force Base) in Ohio during early 1944.

Fw 190G Cowling Development

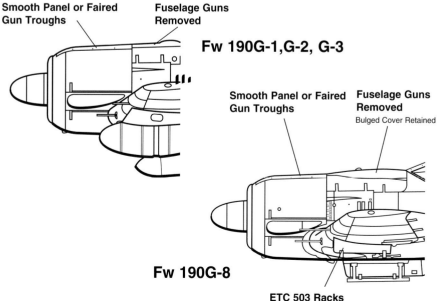

Smooth Panel or Faired Gun Troughs

Fuselage Guns Removed

Fw 190G-1, G-2, G-3

Smooth Panel or Faired Gun Troughs

Fuselage Guns Removed
Bulged Cover Retained

Fw 190G-8

ETC 503 Racks

FW 190G-8

The Fw 190G-8 was a contemporary of the Fw 190A-8 and F-8 series, also entering production in 1944. Externally, the G-8 looked like the F-8, but the fuselage machine guns were removed, although the bulged fuselage armament panel was usually retained. Armament, as with all Fw 190Gs was restricted to the wing root MG 151 20mm cannons. Like the A-8 and F-8 models, the Fw 190G-8 was further identifiable by its outboard positioned pitot tube. Along with the usual fuselage ETC 501 ventral rack, the Fw 190G-8 was equipped with two underwing ETC 503 racks, which were streamlined and, like the Fw 190G-3, allowed the Fw 190G-8 to carry either 300 liter underwing fuel tanks or bombs. Many later examples were fitted with 'blown hoods', while others were equipped with 'fluted' exhaust dampers for nocturnal missions.

As the borders of the Reich shrank closer to Germany, long-range missions became of less importance, resulting in the installation of four underwing ETC 71 bomb racks (to carry four 50kg bombs) under the designation Fw 190G-8/R5. This *Rüstsätze* was reportedly applied to surviving Fw 190G-3s if needed. When fully loaded, the Fw 190G-8 achieved a weight of 5,200 kg (11,463.9 lbs) with a combat range of approximately 1,125 km (699 miles). These figures are reportedly based on a flying condition of a fuselage 300 liter fuel tank and maximum underwing bomb load, if not a triple bomb load. In a fully loaded condition, the G-8's speed was reduced to approximately 450 km/h (279 mph).

Of the Fw 190G-8s manufactured (precise numbers are unknown), most were assigned to ground attack units along the collapsing Eastern and Western Fronts, serving alongside other close support variants of the Fw 190. Although a further G variant was planned, the Fw 190G-10, it failed to progress beyond design stages due to the war situation.

With the exception of its fuselage-mounted guns, this aircraft (which has been identified as different variants) demonstrates features of the Fw 190G-8, including the streamlined ETC 503 underwing racks and a wing tip pitot tube. Like the Fw 190A-8 from which it was adapted, the G-8 also featured a bulged fuselage armament panel. The tropical air intakes were optional. (Hans Redeman)

Fw 190G Wing Details

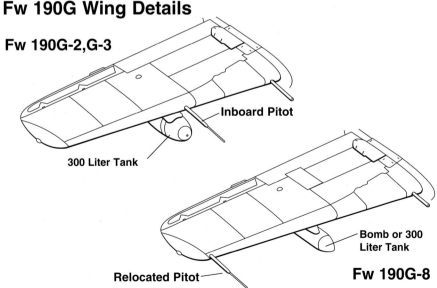

Fw 190G-2,G-3

Inboard Pitot

300 Liter Tank

Relocated Pitot

Bomb or 300 Liter Tank

Fw 190G-8

The wing tip pitot tube indicates that this machine is either an Fw 190G-8 or possibly an Fw 190A-8 *Nacht Jabo-Rei* (without a clear view of the underwing racks, the two variants were otherwise externally identical). The wing ETC 503 racks of the Fw 190G-8 could carry bombs or 300 liter drop tanks as seen here. The G-8 could also be equipped with fluted flame dampers on the exhausts, which are just visible behind the cowling.

FW 190 TORPEDO CARRIERS

It became a passion of the RLM to attempt the conversion of existing aircraft types into torpedo-bombers, particularly since the *Luftwaffe* possessed no dedicated torpedo carrying machines. Accordingly, the Fw 190 underwent its share of torpedo modifications, using both factory conversions (*Umrüst-Bausätzen*) and field ready conversions (*Rüstsätzen*). These torpedo carrying developments spanned the last two years of the war, beginning with the Fw 190A-5, and ultimately involving later Fw 190F variants. Success with the Fw 190 torpedo bombers was limited, with some proving to have disappointing performance. Those which reportedly did see combat, did so using mostly lighter caliber *bomben-torpedos* (BT), such as the BT 400 and BT 700 series weapons. In the event, most of the Luftwaffe's torpedo attack missions fell upon two twin-engined stalwarts, the Heinkel He 111 and the Junkers Ju 88. Fw 190 torpedo bomber development involved the following types:

Fw 190A-5/U14 A factory prototype for carrying an LTF5b torpedo on a fuselage ETC 502 ventral rack. The aircraft, coded TD+SI (WNr.871), produced unfavorable results and was eventually abandoned. It was also modified with an extended rear undercarriage leg for load clearance and an enlarged vertical fin and rudder in an attempt to improve handling qualities.

Fw 190A-5/U15 A single factory prototype for an improved torpedo carrier with a PKS 11 automatic-pilot system. A modified ETC 501 fuselage rack allowed for the carrying of lighter

torpedo loads. Experiments were also conducted with the Blohm und Voss Bv 246 *Hagelkorn* glider bomb.

Fw 190F-8/R14, R15 and **R16** *Rüstsätzen* Test bed aircraft for several torpedo loads. Various installations were proposed for carrying the LTF5b torpedo on an ETC 502 fuselage rack (R14), a centerline BT 1400 torpedo-bomb with an ETC 502 rack (R15), a centerline BT 700 torpedo-bomb with an ETC 501 rack (R16) or two underwing BT 400 torpedo-bombs on ETC 503 racks. Modifications were also tested with the undercarriage, reduced defensive weapons, and enlarged vertical tail surfaces.

Fw 190F-8/U2, U3, U4 and **U5** Proposed factory converted torpedo-bombers, testing similar equipment and weapons variations to the Fw 190F-8/R14 through R16 series.

Fw 190F-16/R14 A proposed project which was to feature a BMW 801TJ 1,810 hp engine and an ETC 802 or ETC 804 fuselage rack for larger torpedoes, such as the LTF5b. Other proposed refinements included a four-bladed VDM propeller and expanded vertical tail surfaces. The deteriorating war situation caused this project as well as many others to be cancelled.

Torpedo Types

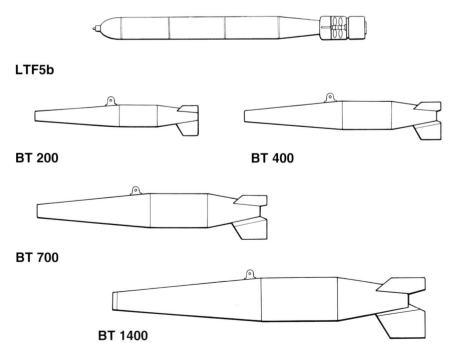

LTF5b

BT 200

BT 400

BT 700

BT 1400

TD+SI (WNr. 871) was the first torpedo carrying Fw 190, under the designation Fw 190A-5/U14. It carried an LTF5b torpedo on an ETC 502 rack and was equipped with an extended tail undercarriage leg and expanded vertical tail surfaces. Its poor performance led to its cancellation. (Hans Redeman)

The drag produced by the large ETC 502 rack and torpedo can be imagined. The extended tail wheel leg did not allow for complete retraction which also caused drag. Despite the failure of this modification, a similar installation was tested on the Fw 190F-8/R14, but with a smaller ETC 502 rack.

On post war display in England, this Fw 190F-8/R15 reportedly was once assigned to the special operations unit III *Gruppe/KG* 200. Similar to the original A-5/U14, it was rigged with an extended tail leg and an ETC 502 fuselage rack. Its limited missions were believed to have been restricted to using the BT series torpedo-bombs (BT 700 or BT 1400), or standard bomb loads. (Imperial War Museum)

VARIANTS

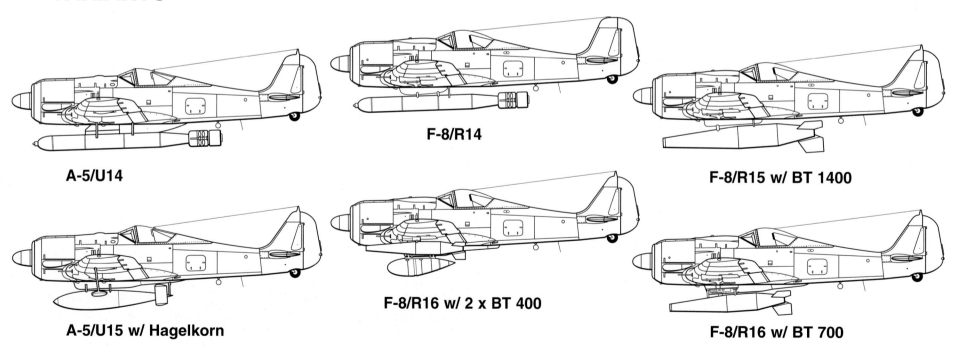

A-5/U14

F-8/R14

F-8/R15 w/ BT 1400

A-5/U15 w/ Hagelkorn

F-8/R16 w/ 2 x BT 400

F-8/R16 w/ BT 700

FW 190 TRAINERS

The prospect of creating a two-seat Fw 190 for pilot conversion training (which had been proposed earlier in the war) had taken on an added importance by 1943 when bomber pilots, especially those assigned to the *Stuka* units, required quick and easy retraining to the Fw 190 ground attack variants. Some of the first conversions involved the use of Fw 190A-5s, which were stripped of armament and fitted with an aft extension of the canopy to house an instructor's cockpit. It is believed that this variant was assigned the provisional designation of A-5/U1, which conflicts with an armament test-bed given the same title. However, it was not unusual for a designation to be re-assigned after the project was terminated.

Following the introduction of the Fw 190A-8 in early 1944, a two-seat version was assigned the factory designation of Fw 190A-8/U1, the extended rear canopy being similar to that of the two seat A-5 version. In the event, both variants came to be known as the Fw 190S-5 and Fw 190S-8 (S for *Schulflugzeug*). The S-8 could be distinguished from the S-5 by the retention of its bulged fuselage armament panel, although it also was unarmed. Some S-8s also featured a lateral extension of the aft windows, using triangular flat transparencies, to improve the instructor's forward vision. Ultimately, only a handful of both variants were manufactured, beginning in June of 1944, and were issued to training units and a few operational combat units as required.

Surviving Fw 190S aircraft found by the Allies at war's end carried a variety of camouflage schemes, often with simplified national markings. One damaged Fw 190S-5 wearing full Eastern Front markings was credited to *Schlachtgeschwader* 151. Small lettering behind the canopy displayed the machine's *Werke Nummer* (W.Nr. 2541) and a manufacturing date of 29 June 1944. Although Fw 190S trainers were based primarily on A-5 and A-8 airframes, the sole remaining example, currently on display in England, features a manufacturer's data plate describing it as an Fw 190F-8/U1.

Fw 190S-5

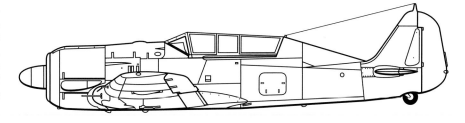

Fw 190S-8

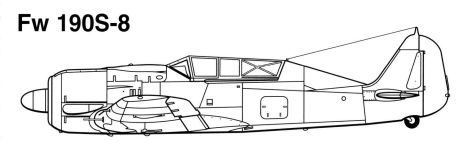

The last shot has been fired. With their propellers and rudders removed to prevent unauthorized flights, this post war collection of Fw 190s is earmarked for destruction. Most appear to have been used as trainers, particularly the two-seat Fw 190A-8/U1 (Fw 190S-8) which is second to last in line. Barely discernable is its fuselage code of Q+7. (Imperial War Museum)

More Aircraft of the Luftwaffe and its Allies in WW II

1044 Messerschmitt Bf 109, Pt 1

1057 Messerschmitt Bf 109, Pt 2

1073 Ju 87 Stuka

1142 Fw 189

1147 Me 210/410

1159 Heinkel He 112

6069 Hungarian Air Force

5510 Fw 190D Walk Around

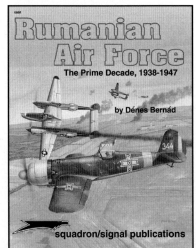

6080 Rumanian Air Force